ABORTION

The Ultimate Exploitation of Women

ABORTION

The Ultimate Exploitation of Women

Brian Fisher

BROWN CHRISTIAN PRESS
A DIVISION OF
BROWN BOOKS PUBLISHING

Abortion
The Ultimate Exploitation of Women

Brown Christian Press
16250 Knoll Trail Drive, Suite 205
Dallas, Texas 75248
www.BrownChristianPress.com
(972) 381-0009

A New Era in Publishing®

ISBN 978-1-61254-948-4
LCCN 2016953364

Printed in the United States
10 9 8 7 6 5 4 3 2 1

For more information or to contact the author, please go to www.HumanCoalition.org.

Contents

Acknowledgments

I first met Dr. Tim Boswell over e-mail and phone in 2014. His collaboration and editing prowess made one of my previous books, *Deliver Us From Abortion*, so much better than what I had originally drafted, so I asked him to help me craft this next edition of *Abortion: The Ultimate Exploitation of Women*. Once again he has outdone himself, taking my rough thoughts and copy and refining them into something readable. Though we've only met in person twice over the past two years, he is a kindred spirit, both in his passion for humanity and his desire to use the written word to change hearts and minds.

John Aman assisted me greatly with the first version of this book, and I continue to owe him a debt of gratitude.

To the directors, advisory board, and selfless donors of Human Coalition, for their staunch support of our work.

To the growing, vibrant, deeply committed staff and volunteers of Human Coalition; you have my deepest gratitude for your tireless work and relentless pursuit of the end of abortion.

To my best friend and wife, Jessica, for her candor, humor, and support. And to our sons, Caleb and Zach, both fine young men. May you follow the legacy of many other men who refuse to treat women as anything less than equals and who give all to protect the lives and humanity of the youngest of our race.

To those contributors who courageously shared their abortion and life stories with me—thank you for your transparency and willingness to see others positively impacted by your experiences.

Notes on Version 2 of *Abortion: The Ultimate Exploitation of Women*

It might seem somewhat presumptive to release a second version of a book that never hit the *New York Times* bestseller list. I'm not sure a book about abortion, women's rights, gender equality, feminism, and man's failings will ever sell tens of thousands of copies. It's not exactly a book that many people want to read.

When the first version was released in 2013, I had hoped that a few men would read it and feel compelled to engage in the quest to end abortion in America. Men certainly read it. And so did women.

I did the normal things authors do when peddling books—I used social media, radio interviews, TV, and a few book signings to promote the book. And when the feedback began to come in, I was surprised by what I learned.

The number-one comment I got from the first version, from both men and women, was: "I just didn't know. I didn't know the history of abortion, men's role in spreading it, and the degree to which it has ripped apart the fabric of the American family."

I've even heard from pastors, several of whom were provoked to start educating their flocks about the damage inflicted by abortion.

And so the book became a primer of sorts for people who wanted to understand the abortion epidemic better. The book was download-ed for free over thirty-five thousand times worldwide and took on a life I could never have anticipated. It was translated into Spanish and Romanian and has been used in various countries to educate their populations.

Over the last three years, however, I realized that the original version was missing some key components and needed to be updated—which it has been, with over one hundred new sources cited and countless others brought up to date. In the first version, I had not fully developed how men can, are, and should be a part of ending abortion. I had not presented a complete picture of how men target and exploit women globally and how this oppression is deeply connected to abortion. And I missed a wonderful opportunity to share some stories from men who triumphed over past mistakes and failures to become warriors on behalf of women and their children.

Though abortion was born in America primarily because of men, abortion is dying in America because men are, in fact, joining women in the fight to make it history. And women, men, and children are infinitely better off because of it.

This isn't the easiest book to read, and I deeply appreciate your taking the time to do so. I think this version retains an accurate historical perspective, tells a more complete story, and ends, appropriately, with a far more hopeful outlook.

Brian Fisher

Summer 2016

Introduction:
"Your Book Title Makes No Sense"

Abortion: The Ultimate Exploitation of Women.

That's a ridiculous title, isn't it?

Abortion doesn't exploit women—it empowers them. Abortion is a legal right for women that permits them to do whatever they want with their own bodies. Abortion has freed women from the bonds of male dominance and biological slavery. It has narrowed the gender gap and elevated the value and role of women in American society.

Abortion is choice, and choice is power.

Men Started It. Men Oppress With It. Men Can End It.

And what's this about men? They use abortion to oppress women? That's just crazy. Why would men promote abortion? They don't even have the legal right to influence the abortion decision. Socially, they aren't even really allowed to talk about it.

We are told that abortion has nothing to do with men. It is a huge step forward for women's rights.

There are three very good reasons why this should be true:

1. Abortion is legal in the United States, and that law empowers women. The landmark 1973 *Roe v. Wade* case effectively stripped men of any legal right to protect or terminate the life of a child in the womb. The Supreme Court decided the right to abort rests solely

with women. It found that right in the Fourteenth Amendment and acknowledged that it might also be found in the Ninth.[1] What it didn't find was any legal authority for a father to have a say about the fate of his offspring.

In two subsequent abortion cases, the Court threw out a law requiring the husband's consent to his wife's abortion and another mandating that he be notified when his wife was on her way to an abortion facility. As the Court put it in the latter case, "[I]t cannot be claimed that the father's interest in the fetus' welfare is equal to the mother's protected liberty. . . ."[2] So far as the Court is concerned, men have no rights whatsoever with respect to their preborn progeny. The so-called right to privacy, as the Court said in *Roe*, "is broad enough to encompass a woman's decision whether or not to terminate her pregnancy"[3]—and to terminate the father's rights, as well.

2. Abortion is a surgical procedure that, for obvious reasons, only involves the female body. Because women are entrusted with providing sustenance and proper living conditions for a developing, in-utero human being, any changes to that process must be carried out within the woman's body. Abortion is a surgical procedure that cannot be performed on men. Thus, men should not be able to dictate whether or not the surgical procedure is performed on women.

3. In America today, 40 percent of all births are out of wedlock.[4] With 24 percent of mothers raising kids without a father present[5] and over 80 percent of all single-parent households being led by single mothers,[6] women are increasingly responsible not only for carrying a child during pregnancy—but for fully providing for that child once she is born.

We often speak of abortion in biological terms, constraining the conversation to life inside the womb. But the implications of raising a child after birth are very much a part of the abortion decision. In the Supreme Court's ruling in *Roe v. Wade*, it considered this fact when it noted that raising the child may "force upon the woman a distressful life and future," due to possible "[p]sychological harm," "[m]ental and physical health" taxation, and the possible "stigma of unwed motherwood."[7]

If the father of the child has abandoned the pregnant mother, she is now put in a very difficult position. She carries the emotional and physical weight of carrying the child before birth, and she now can anticipate a drastic change to her lifestyle, expenses, and social status after her child's birth.

The impact on lifestyle, finances, and timing are the three primary reasons women choose to abort in America today. A 2004 study conducted by researchers at the Guttmacher Institute—a proabortion organization—asked 1,209 women why they obtained abortions.

The reasons most frequently given: "Having a baby would dramatically change my life" and "I can't afford a baby now" (cited by 74 and 73 percent, respectively).[8]

Another study, published in 2013 in *BMC Women's Health*, polled 954 women from thirty abortion facilities across the United States and found similar results; although these women gave multiple reasons rather than a sole factor, the two most commonly given reasons fell under "Not financially prepared" concerns (40 percent) and timing issues such as "Bad timing/not ready/unplanned," "Too busy/not enough time," or "Too old" (36 percent).[9]

Since more and more men are leaving pregnant women without financial, emotional, or physical help, the decision to abort should rest with the gender responsible for the entire process. Author Kathleen McDonnell summarizes this view succinctly: "Women are the ones who bear children. Women are the ones, still, who are largely responsible for their care and nurturing. It is our bodies and our lives that are at issue, so the decisions must be ours as well."[10]

In a column responding to high-school boys who petitioned her on behalf of the preborn child, *Cleveland's Plain Dealer* writer Connie Schultz put it another way: "How do these boys figure that a woman's womb is any of their business? How do men, for that matter?"[11]

Indeed, how is it possible that choosing abortion is anything *but* an empowering decision for women? If the Supreme Court supports the woman's right to choose, biology mandates abortion only be performed on women, and women are increasingly being abandoned by men in the child-rearing process, why should men have any say at all?

For many men, it's just fine that they don't have the right to say anything. Their goal of using women to achieve their own selfish purposes has already been achieved. They now enjoy a new kind of freedom—a new kind of emancipation—because of a "woman's right to choose."

These "purposes" have very little to do with empowering women. In fact, man's relentless promotion of abortion exploits women in the most personal, debilitating, and disrespectful way. It is yet another tool to persecute and diminish women, pushing them farther away from gender equality. In the process, men are doing enormous damage to the physical and emotional well-being of millions of American women and their families.

And men walk away from the damage with no responsibility or accountability. In fact, we are able to give the same passive rationalization we've been giving for millennia: "It's her fault. It's her responsibility. Not mine."

How is it, then, that our culture celebrates abortion as a woman's choice? It's her body; it's her life. If men are behind the abortion issue, why is it that women are taking full responsibility for the choice and its consequences?

The answer is simple: that's exactly what proabortion men want our culture to think.

Early feminists were passionately against abortion, understanding that abortion exploited and harmed women.

In fact, I didn't invent the book title *The Ultimate Exploitation of Women*. The original architect of the Equal Rights Amendment coined the phrase to describe abortion and its impact on females. Her name was Alice Paul, and she was a feminist.

But time, money, effective marketing, and persuasive messaging have changed the culture. We bought the lie. And while men achieve their social and personal goals, millions of women are victimized, yet celebrate their own exploitation and call it a right.

Women aren't the only victims of abortion. There are many thousands of men who, today, continue to mourn the loss of children they had no legal right to protect. And there are untold family members of both genders who have been deeply wounded by abortion.

And, of course, there are about 60 million human beings of both genders who have lost their lives to abortion—the most innocent victims of all.

If you are a postabortive woman who regrets having an abortion, it's important for you to know that I (and thousands of others) do not hold you in contempt. In fact, mercy, compassion, and grace are extended to you, and I hope you have found it or are on your way to doing so.

If you are a postabortive man with regrets, know that I've spent time with men who lost children to abortion and are now deeply hurt because of it. In many cases, it was your pressure, passivity, or pocketbook that caused it. In some cases, you desperately wanted to keep your child and had no legal right to do so. Either way, you lost. There is hope and healing for you, also, and I pray you find it.

If you are a postabortive woman who does not regret the abortion decision and continues to favor abortion rights, there is no contempt for you. Abortion is legal, and you exercised your legal right to abort. I urge you, though, to confront the reality of the aftereffects of abortion and its horrific impact on society and your gender. And I will challenge your premise that abortion furthers gender equality. It does not. You are being manipulated in ways that are terribly unfair and unjust to women.

If you are a man who favors abortion (postabortive or not), I challenge you to read this book and consider its facts. My hope is that you will at least take responsibility for your role and acknowledge the degrading impact abortion has on women, men, the family, and society. Your active or passive promotion of abortion is destroying the fabric of what makes America great. This isn't opinion. It is fact.

And for those men who claim they support life and true gender equality, I say this: abortion will not be ended in America until you *do* something. As someone who sat on the sidelines for years, doing nothing to protect women and the preborn from abortion, I urge you to read this book and take action. As Dietrich Bonhoeffer stated, "Silence in the face of evil is itself evil. . . . Not to speak is to speak. Not to act is to act."

Just as abortion was wrought on America by men, it will only be ended in America when men stand beside women, as equals, to cooperatively rid America of the death and suffering.

Don't just sit there and say you affirm life. Saying you affirm life but doing nothing makes you irrelevant. Don't wait passively on the sidelines, hoping for change. The stakes are too high.

One Housekeeping Note

I do not use the term "pro-choice" in this book unless it is a quotation. I use the term "proabortion," "abortion advocate," or "abortion proponent." This is not because I am attempting to upset those who favor abortion. It is because the term "pro-choice" is misleading and incorrect.

There is a widely held belief that one can be pro-choice and not proabortion. This means that a person supports the right to choose abortion but generally wishes abortion wouldn't happen.

To be "pro-choice" means one is in favor of having options or choices. To be "proabortion" means one is in favor of the legality and practice of abortion.

I am as pro-choice as it gets. I am in favor of a woman having a myriad of options: where to go to college, what career to pursue, whether or not she wants to get married, whom she marries, whom to vote for, whether or not she wants to run a business, what she wants to do with her free time, whether or not to enter politics, etc.

7

However, I do not believe that any person, whether male or female, should have the option to take the life of another innocent human being.

The term "pro-choice" was invented in the mid-1970s to avoid using the term "proabortion," a designation which "in the pre-*Roe* years had served as the standard label for a person in favor of legalization [of abortion]."[12] Former abortionist Bernard Nathanson, a founding member of NARAL (National Association for the Repeal of Abortion Laws), the group that led efforts to legalize abortion, called "pro-choice" a "Madison Avenue euphemism."[13]

The goal of this effort by abortion activists to "remake the vocabulary with which Americans talked about abortion," as abortion historian Cynthia Gorney described it,[14] was to take attention off the abortion procedure and loss of life and instead make the issue about women's rights.

But to be in favor of the choice to take a life is to be in support of the practice of doing so. One could argue that to be offered the choice to abort is not the same as actually aborting. But one's permission to do something is condoning and, therefore, supporting that practice.

The opposite of pro-life is not pro-choice; it's proabortion—in favor of the practice of abortion. If you think abortion should be safe and rare, or only available in cases of rape or incest, or something to be used as a last resort, you are still proabortion.

My goal in writing this book is to shed light on the victimization of women, showing that the female gender is under attack in America. While I am life affirming, I am also a proponent of true equal rights for both genders, and that is the focus of this book.

Ending abortion in America would not just benefit the millions of children who lose their lives each year. It would be an enormous step forward for women in their appropriate quest for equal rights and equal protection. And, if men would be so convicted, ending the practice would likewise be a great leap ahead in their efforts to live out their appropriate roles as selfless partners, serving alongside women for their shared and mutual good.

CHAPTER 1
Just a Women's Issue?

There is no topic as heated, controversial, and emotional in America today as abortion. It seems everyone has an opinion on it, and expressing those opinions is likely to start a lively, impassioned debate.

In many cases, though, we don't talk about it. Abortion has entered the cultural realm of "religion" and "politics"—subjects we don't discuss in the company of family, coworkers, and strangers. It's too awkward, too personal, too heavy, and will likely invite conflict we want to avoid. Oddly enough, like religion and politics, abortion touches every American and is deeply embedded in the cultural fabric of our existence. It's fascinating how we like to avoid talking about the subjects most important to us.

I've tested the premise that people don't like to talk about abortion, and the anecdotal results are sometimes humorous, sometimes sad, sometimes frustrating.

The conversation may go like this: "So, Brian, what do you do for a living?"

"I work to rescue children and families from abortion."

Once in a while, someone will respond with great enthusiasm, eager to hear about that work.

Too often, though, people will look aside. I have learned what that means. They are postabortive and have just been reminded of it. Sometimes they will tell me their story, but most of the time they quickly change the conversation. I suspect most postabortive people expect me to be judgmental and think ill of them. That's not the case, as I have too often seen the intense pain and shame abortion brings. Abortion creates all sorts of victims.

Sometimes a person will immediately change the subject and go to great lengths to make sure we don't come back around to that particular topic. That generally means someone is highly in favor of abortion and doesn't want to get into a discussion about it.

It is rare that someone actually engages in a conversation about abortion in America.

Yet abortion has saturated our culture and pervades nearly every area of our lives. Statistics suggest every family in America has been touched by abortion in some way or other.

Abortion Impacts Everyone

Consider just a few brief facts:

- Abortion is one of the most common surgical procedures in the United States.
- It is the leading cause of death (heart disease kills 600,000 annually while over 1 million preborn children die each year from abortion).[15]
- Almost 60 million Americans have lost their lives to abortion since 1973.
- Three in ten women in America are postabortive by the time they are forty-five.[16] This implies that around 30 percent of men are also postabortive. (Postabortive means, if you are a woman,

that you've had an abortion. If you are a man, it means you are the father of an aborted child.)

- Abortion is an enormous industry, generating more than $800 million[17] each year for abortion doctors, facilities, and providers. Black-market industries exist around the business of abortion.[18]

- Virtually every major city in America has at least one abortion clinic. Most large cities have several.

- Pharmaceutical abortions (abortions using a pill such as RU-486) continue to rise in popularity.

- There are thousands of nonprofit organizations attempting to reduce or eliminate abortion, and there are numerous such organizations promoting it. There is no shortage of ink spilled over the abortion issue online, in magazines, and in the papers. It is a constant topic on TV, whether in our pop culture (*16 and Pregnant*) or in the news.

- Our political candidates typically declare a formal position on the topic before every election.

Over the past forty years, abortion has become part of our families, part of our communities, and part of our culture.

If abortion is so pervasive and common, can it really just be a women's issue?

The mainstream media and proabortion organizations continue to assert as much. Planned Parenthood, the largest abortion provider in the United States, celebrated the fortieth anniversary of *Roe v. Wade* by stating, "That's 40 years of protecting every woman's fundamental right to make her own personal medical decisions."

Since *Roe v. Wade* effectively supports that assertion, it's no surprise that many men and women fully support it, especially in politics and entertainment:

"I remain committed to protecting a woman's right to choose and this fundamental constitutional right. . . . [W]e must also continue our efforts to ensure that our daughters have the same rights, freedoms, and opportunities as our sons to fulfill their dreams."

—President Barack Obama[19]

"I don't want to turn back the hands of time to when women shuttled across state lines in the thick of night to resolve an unwanted pregnancy, in a cheap hotel room just south of the state line. Where a transaction of $600 cash becomes the worth of a young woman's life."

—Mark Ruffalo[20]

"Being pro-choice is trusting the individual to make the right decision for herself and her family, and not entrusting that decision to anyone wearing the authority of government in any regard."

—Hillary Clinton[21]

"Ten years old. That's the age my child would have been. And I would not be here in Glasgow. I would not be in this band or traveling. . . . Yeah, there are programs to assist. Welfare and health programs that are constant victims of cutbacks. The child can sit in severely overcrowded classrooms and be taught by underpaid teachers. A right to a healthy future should be the consideration."

—Eddie Vedder[22]

"The people who say that we shouldn't have the right to choose, that the government should interfere with our womb, are not people who believe in helping mothers who are poor or psychologically or emotionally unfit or unable to have children. . . ."

—Jane Fonda[23]

"Can small-minded idiot blokes stop telling women whether or not they're entitled to abortions please?"

—Lily Allen[24]

"Much like the pro-lifers, I believe in protecting the child—when she's being forced to have a baby at 14."

—Sarah Silverman[25]

"Reproductive choice is a fundamental human right and we can never take it for granted. On this issue, you're either with us or against us."

—former New York mayor Michael Bloomberg[26]

"We are deeply disturbed by . . . the growing movement to limit women's reproductive rights. And as Mother's Day approaches, we join Planned Parenthood in their fight to protect women . . . across the country."

—Gwyneth Paltrow and Blythe Danner[27]

"A pile of goop should not have more rights than a human being. Period."

—Lucas Neff (star of Fox's *Raising Hope*)[28]

"I support the Supreme Court decision that says an abortion is a woman's decision, very difficult decision, to be made privately in conjunction with her religious beliefs, her doctor, her responsibility to her family— and the government is completely inappropriate in that decision."

—Susan Sarandon[29]

Abortion Impacts Men

But is abortion really just about females? Is it just about their bodies, their choices, and their rights? Or is there something else going on beneath the surface?

Obviously, the act of abortion impacts both genders. Both males and females lose their lives in the womb.

Though there are numerous arguments about when a preborn child is a person or should have rights, there is no longer any rational disagreement about when human life begins. Human life begins at conception. A unique, completely distinct human being is wonderfully created at conception. She has all of the genetic material she needs to continue to mature through the phases of pregnancy, birth, and beyond.

The purpose of this book is not to exhaustively argue the topic of "personhood" (which is dealt with fairly by Robert George and Christopher Tollefsen in their book, *Embryo: A Defense of Human Life*), though the topic will arise in later chapters. The process of assigning value to a human life at some point beyond conception is subjective and variable. Science has proven that life begins at conception—and that life is a member of the species *Homo sapiens*, a human being.

As prominent scholar and author Stanley Fish has stated, "Pro-life arguments are now based on scientific evidence and the pro-choice arguments are not. That is a cultural, historical fact."[30] Scientists have been supporting this conclusion for decades, as a quick tour of medical textbooks and scholarly works over the years shows:

1970s:

"The development of a human being begins with fertilization, a process by which two highly specialized cells, the spermatozoon from the male and the oocyte from the female, unite to give rise to a new organism, the *zygote*."[31]

"Embryo: The developing individual. . . . At the moment the sperm cell of the human male meets the ovum of the female and the union results in a fertilized ovum (zygote), a new life has begun. . . ."[32]

1980s:

An embryology textbook describes how birth is just an event in the development of a baby, not the beginning of his/her life: "It should always be remembered that many organs are still not completely developed by full-term and birth should be regarded only as an incident in the whole developmental process."[33]

"Human development begins after the union of male and female gametes or germ cells during a process known as *fertilization* (conception). . . .This fertilized ovum, known as a *zygote*, is a large diploid cell that is the beginning, or *primordium*, of a human being."[34]

1990s:

"Zygote. This cell, formed by the union of an ovum and a sperm (Gr. *zyg tos*, yoked together), represents the beginning of a human being."[35]

"The development of a human begins with fertilization. . . ."[36]

"Almost all higher animals start their lives from a single cell, the fertilized ovum (zygote). . . . The time of fertilization represents the starting point in the life history, or ontogeny, of the individual."[37]

2000–Present:

"Human life begins at fertilization, the process during which a male gamete or sperm (spermatozoo development) unites with a female gamete or oocyte (ovum) to form a single cell called a zygote. This highly specialized, totipotent cell marked the beginning of each of us as a unique individual."[38]

"Fertilization is the process by which male and female haploid gametes (sperm and egg) unite to produce a genetically distinct individual."[39]

The government's own definition attests to the fact that life begins at fertilization. According to the National Institutes of Health, "fertilization" is the process of union of two gametes (i.e., ovum and sperm) "whereby the somatic chromosome number is restored and the development of a new individual is initiated."[40]

Thus abortion is, by definition, the willful termination of a human life. Very few abortion proponents today argue otherwise—mainly because the facts of life are conclusive.

Given that the sex ratio at conception is estimated to be fifty-fifty between male and female human beings,[41] it stands to reason that around half of the 60 million babies aborted in America over the last forty-plus years were male. Abortion most certainly impacts the male gender.

Ironically, though males are aborted, the procedure disproportionately culls preborn females through sex-selection abortions. Some 200 million girls worldwide are missing[42] due to this practice, which takes place even in the United States.[43]

However, not every human being who is aborted dies. There are numerous cases of "abortion survivors," human beings who were aborted, didn't die, and were then born. Many of those survivors are male.

Take Josiah Presley, for instance. Josiah was aborted by his mother in South Korea but survived. He was eventually adopted by parents in the United States and is a perfectly normal young man (save his left arm, which was presumably damaged in the abortion attempt).

Other men are alive today because their mothers, though encouraged to abort, chose, instead, to carry their babies. Singer, entertainer, and TV personality Nick Cannon and NFL quarterback Tim Tebow are both examples of grown men saved from potential death in the womb by their own mothers. Actor and filmmaker Jack Nicholson is another. Nicholson—who is the most-nominated male actor in the history of the Academy Awards—has stated that his stance against abortion is due to being born out of wedlock himself.

His mother, a showgirl, became pregnant with him as a teenager and was encouraged to have an abortion but did not.[44] In a 1984 interview with *Rolling Stone*, Nicholson stated about abortion, "I'm positively against it. I don't have the right to any other view."[45] In another interview two years later, he elaborated: "It's an open-and-shut case where I'm concerned. As an illegitimate child born in 1937, during the Depression, to a broken lower-middle-class family, you are a candidate for—you're an automatic abortion with most people today. So it's very easy for me."[46]

Other men were saved from abortion even though their mothers were raped. Activist and media expert Ryan Bomberger is alive today because his mother, who was raped, chose to carry Ryan and place him for adoption.[47]

All of these men have strong opinions about abortion, and their existence proves men have been profoundly influenced by it.

Should these men be silenced because of the impact abortion has had on them personally? Should men be silent when tens of millions of male humans have perished in the womb?

Mars and Venus Actually Agree

Much is made in the media about abortion as a dividing line between men and women. But the so-called "gender gap" on abortion—based on the idea that this is a women's issue—doesn't exist. Men and women think alike on abortion.

A 2013 Pew Poll found "no gender gap in opinions about *Roe v. Wade*: Nearly identical percentages of women (64 percent) and men (63 percent) oppose reversing the decision."[48] Concerning late-term abortion, a 2014 Quinnipiac University national poll similarly found gender agreement in that 61 percent of men and 59 percent of women would support legislation banning abortions after twenty weeks of pregnancy, except in cases of rape or incest.[49]

The real split over abortion falls along religious lines. Fifty percent of people who attend religious services at least weekly want *Roe* overturned, while just 17 percent of those who attend worship less than weekly favor *Roe*'s reversal.[50]

"You Can Speak Your Mind . . . As Long as We Agree"

Men are welcomed to take a position favoring abortion. They are even welcomed to take a neutral, passive stance. But they are not welcomed to take a public stance for life. If they do, they are derided and accused of being antiwoman, anti-reproductive rights, and traditionalist. Sometimes just being a man makes you suspect to proabortion feminists, which is why attorney and activist Florynce Kennedy once cracked, "If men could get pregnant, abortion would be a sacrament."[51]

The organization I work for, Human Coalition (formerly Online for Life), released an iPhone app that allows people to pray for families considering abortion. One woman reviewed the app and wrote, "I have aborted several babies from my uterus. When did they [men at Human Coalition] get vaginas? Oh wait. They didn't. Good luck with this bologna."

Another wrote, "Hey Brian, how completely self-righteous of you to proclaim you know what's best for anyone but yourself. Especially in the cases of pregnant women, considering you'll never experience pregnancy and don't know their circumstances. This app is crazy town. Mind your own business."

The point is this: because the abortion procedure is performed on a woman's body, men have no right to opine or intrude.

What abortion defenders say, in effect, is "You can't get pregnant, so leave the abortion issue to women," as life-affirming debater Scott Klusendorf points out. The fact is, arguments don't have genders. They're either true or false, regardless of whether they are made by a man or a woman.

If, as some have argued, the qualification for addressing the abortion issue is the ability to bear children, then *Roe* itself is thrown into question, and all the men who legalized abortion and work in the abortion advocacy business ought to look for work elsewhere. Seven of the nine men on the Supreme Court voted for the legalization of abortion. Should their votes not have counted because they didn't have uteruses? What about the numerous men who work for Planned Parenthood, the ACLU, and other proabortion organizations? Should their voices be counted?

In fact, they are heard. The only voices not allowed to speak are those of men who are not in favor of abortion. As Klusendorf points out, the argument ought to be restated, "No man can speak on abortion unless he agrees with us."[52]

Prostate cancer kills thousands of men each year. Men care very much about prostate cancer, and they should have access to resources in order to be properly educated, so they can avoid getting it. Does that mean that women, who don't have male organs, have no right to talk about prostate cancer? Or do both genders agree that prostate cancer kills men?

For that matter, obstetrician-gynecologists practice medicine that exclusively involves women and their bodies. Should only female OB/GYNs be allowed to discuss their field, share their research, or voice concerns about controversial issues? Are we going to segregate our arguments so that only those sharing the same anatomy (or skin color, or age, or any other factor) can join the discussion, or can we all agree that this is a dangerous and immoral approach—whether we are discussing immigration, human trafficking, abortion, or any other topic?

Facts are facts. A person's gender does not change those facts or reduce one's right to discuss them.

Men as Victims

We are inclined to accept that women should be the only gender with an opinion, right, and authority to choose abortion. After all, they are the ones who experience pregnancy, the abortion itself, and its aftereffects.

Yet more and more evidence suggests that men are also victims of abortion.

Dr. Keith Ablow, a psychiatrist, says he has "listened to dozens of men express lingering, sometimes intense, pain over abortions that proceeded either without their consent, or without them having spoken up about their desires to bring their children to term and parent them."[53]

Shawn Carney, the campaign director of 40 Days for Life, witnessed the anguish of a Korean man unable to prevent his wife from aborting their child. The man begrudgingly drove his wife to an abortion facility in Texas and waited in their parked car with their two young children while his wife went in for her abortion. Carney observed all this while standing outside the clinic fence. After a while, the man left his car and approached Carney with a gut-wrenching appeal. Carney writes:

> [H]e was yelling over and over: "I love children! I love children! Please go get her!" I moved closer to the fence, and he explained to me that he didn't want the abortion. "Please, go get her!" he screamed. "Can't you

do something? I love children!" He pointed desperately to his other two kids in the minivan. "I don't want her abortion. Can't you go in and do something?"

Carney was powerless to help—except to pray—and, ultimately, the man who had been begging Carney to act started to weep in his despair. Unable to stop the death of his own child, he released his grip on the bars of the fence separating the two men and "slid to the ground, his shoulders slumped and heaving."[54]

Another postabortive male, Phil McCombs, a journalist at the *Washington Post*, wrote a public confession, laced with guilt and regret, of the abortion of his child. "I feel like a murderer," McCombs wrote, telling readers that he made sure he was out of town when his partner got the abortion. "I was not by her side to support her. I turned my face away. My behavior was in all respects craven, immoral." The child, whom he came to believe was a boy, "would have inconvenienced me. I'd had my fun. He didn't fit into my plans. . . . His name, which is carved on my heart, was Thomas," he wrote. "I still grieve for little Thomas. It is an ocean of grief."[55]

My dear friend and coworker, Jeff Bradford, knows the pain of abortion first hand:

> I hid and suppressed the realization that the only reason our oldest daughter was not alive today was due to my own cowardice. I went to my wedding, pretending to be an upright, moral young man with my bride dressed all in white. She was beautiful, and we looked great on the outside. No one could see the brokenness we were both hiding so well. We had aborted our first child just a few months before.

For fifteen years, I was too ashamed to tell anyone what I had done, except my best friend. My wife and I never talked about it, we did not grieve together, and we hid it deep in the recesses of our minds. Our marriage began to unravel, and through extensive counseling, we realized how much of our struggle had come down to the decision to end the life of our first child. We began to deal with our own shame and guilt. We realized the extent of the mental and emotional trauma it had caused. There were many levels—resentment, a lack of forgiveness, feelings of abandonment—all revealed as we dealt with the reality of this decision many years earlier.

Now, as a father of four beautiful children, and through God's grace, my wife and I are healing and have been married twenty years. However, there is not a day that goes by that I don't regret my decision. After all, any good father would jump in front of a train to save the life of his child. The life of our first daughter, Sara, should not have been any different.

Not every story has a sad ending, though some are more ironic than others.

While we often associate abortion with a single mother and a deadbeat father, abortion frequently impacts married couples who already have kids. While we may feel disdain for fathers who leave their pregnant partners to pursue the next woman, do we show the same disdain for married men who want to protect and provide for their own preborn children—but have no legal right to do so?

Do we think that a father who has provided a stable, secure home for his family should have no say in the welfare of his own preborn child?

The day after Christmas, a woman, we'll call her Sue, telephoned a local life-affirming center (a community-based organization designed to educate families about pregnancy and options other than abortion). She had already taken two home pregnancy tests—both positive. She had decided to abort her baby. After she had a few questions answered, the woman said she was going to call a few other clinics. The center asked permission to follow up with her in a few days, and she agreed.

Sue called back the next day on her own, asking if she could come in for an ultrasound. She had called abortion clinics, discovered she couldn't get an abortion appointment in her own city for a few weeks, and was preparing to go out of state so she could get the procedure done sooner. Because she needed to verify the pregnancy with an ultrasound before the abortion, she agreed to come into the life-affirming center.

Sue came in that day with her husband, Paul. While she was having her ultrasound, the staff spoke with him.

"I don't want her to get the abortion," Paul said. "I don't like abortion and don't understand why she doesn't want the child."

Sue's reasons were simple. The couple already had a little girl, and she didn't want another baby. She was going to school to get her degree, and another child would make that education very difficult to attain. She wasn't mentally or emotionally ready to be a new mom again.

The center gave her the ultrasound and talked to her about pregnancy, the child, and her options.

The couple left. Paul wanted to have the child; Sue was now unsure if she wanted to abort.

Several days later, the center called Paul to follow up. Paul was over-joyed to report that Sue had changed her mind, and they were going to carry and parent their child.

"I can't thank you enough for talking to her," he said. "I so appreciate your help."

Here's the twist: Paul is a policeman. His job is to protect people, even if it means putting himself in harm's way. Yet he had no legal or cultural authority to protect his own preborn child, whom he desper-ately wanted to live.

The moment his child was born, Paul would have legal rights as a father to do everything possible to protect and provide for his child. And his job requires him to do that for complete strangers every day. Yet, though he wanted his own child to live, he was helpless to protect the baby while she was growing in her mother's womb.

These are just a few examples of the devastating impact abortion has on men—both those who support women in their abortions and those forced to stand and watch while their girlfriends or wives abort their children against their will. The powerlessness imposed on men by the law goes against our very nature as protectors and defenders.

So is abortion just a women's issue? Do the millions of males lost to abortion have a voice? Do postabortive men, who now often suffer in silence, have a voice? Do those men who want to keep their children, but are powerless to stop abortions, have a voice?

Making men sit on the sidelines because it's a "women's issue" conveniently assumes, but does not prove, that the preborn are not members of the human race with the same dignity and right to live as the rest of us. If that unstated assumption is exposed and answered by the facts of science, we're left with a discussion about whether it's right or wrong to kill innocent, vulnerable humans—male and female—at early stages of their development. Men are not only impacted by abortion but obligated to speak up and get involved; this is a human-rights debate, and like every other, one in which women have no monopoly.

But, of course, abortion is legal, so why are we discussing this at all? After all, if the law says it's okay, that means it is right and good. Right?

CHAPTER 2

Our Laws Are Always Right . . . Right?

ncluding abortion in the long list of ways men exploit women may be utterly disagreeable and distasteful to you. Our culture has long accepted that abortion is a woman's right, both socially and legally. How can forty-plus years of law and decades of social education be wrong? How can something that is clearly a woman's right actually be a form of discrimination against women?

You may well argue that abortion is an obvious benefit to women and society. After all, tens of millions of women and men have taken advantage of its availability. If it is legal, how can it be bad for women and families?

Can a right actually be a form of bondage? Can a legal right be wrong?

Indeed, both can be true. Within the last two centuries, another American practice was both legal and socially accepted—but was actually a form of discrimination and bondage.

Dred Scott—Good Law?

Much ink has already been spilled on comparisons between the African slave trade and abortion. My purpose is not to rewrite this discussion—but to illustrate that law and social norms do not always align, and even when they do, they sometimes destroy society, not support it.

Slavery existed for 250 years in America and defined away the humanity and legal status of a whole class of human beings. Like *Roe v. Wade*, it had the Supreme Court's stamp of approval. US Supreme Court Chief Justice Roger B. Taney determined, in the 1857 *Dred Scott* case, that African Americans were "regarded as beings of an inferior order, and altogether unfit to associate with the white race, either in social or political relations, and so far unfit that they had no rights which the white man was bound to respect."[56]

We cringe at the odious racism in Chief Justice Taney's ruling, but the verbiage and tone of that case are strikingly similar to the tone of *Roe v. Wade*. The decision diminishes the preborn, referring to the preborn child as "potential life," and says "meaningful life" may arise later in pregnancy. Justice Harry Blackmun, author of the Opinion of the Court for *Roe*, cites early English common law for this view that it is only later in pregnancy when the "fetus became 'formed' or recognizably human, or . . . when a 'person' came into being. . . ."[57]

Just as the *Dred Scott* ruling was passed despite numerous moral and logical fallacies, there are three key arguments underpinning *Roe v. Wade* that deserve closer examination: the Likelihood argument, the Viability argument, and the Personhood argument.

"Speculative Character": The Likelihood Argument

The 2002 sci-fi movie *Minority Report* wrestles with an ethical conundrum. Tom Cruise plays a police officer who heads up a special unit capable of predicting crimes before they occur. He and his unit (three of whom have the ability to "see" the future) arrest criminals before the crimes are committed, thus rescuing society, reducing violence, and preserving peace and stability. Cruise's character defends this practice until he himself becomes a victim of the system—the unit predicts he will commit a violent crime. He spends the rest of the film running from the system he helped to create.

The film suggests these questions: "Is the best justice system one in which we are guilty until proven innocent? If we could determine guilt before the crime is committed, do we have the right to carry out justice prior to the crime?" The film concludes that the answer to both is *No*—even if we could predict the future, that power is corruptible, and even the most certain future predictions are faulty because of free will. Innocent until proven guilty is the optimal premise for a justice system. We can't judge people for crimes they haven't even committed yet.

The Likelihood argument regarding abortion is a macabre, devious take on *Minority Report*. We don't have "seers" who can see the future. We just have parents, media, and social prognosticators who take their best guess on who should live and die. We don't have an "innocent until proven guilty" approach with preborn humans. They don't have rights, thus they have no opportunity to engage in any justice process.

The Likelihood argument claims that if a mother, family, or American society thinks a preborn child could potentially grow up to be a criminal, or if they could potentially be an economic drain on our social system, we can kill them. No crime has to be committed. No proof of guilt, no proof of economic downturn. Pure conjecture is enough to damn the preborn to death.

This is what happens when we allow an entire class of human beings to be stripped of all rights and privileges. We kill them at will.

The underlying logic behind this position appeared in *Roe v. Wade*. This type of Likelihood argument, based on unknowable contingencies, was in fact specifically criticized by the Supreme Court in their *Roe v. Wade* ruling, but not in relation to Roe. Jane Roe—the pseudonym of a pregnant single woman—was not the only person challenging the constitutionality of a Texas abortion law. As part of the same case, the Does, a childless married couple, also attacked it (not to be confused with the separate Georgia case *Doe v. Bolton*). The Does based alleged injury on the future possibilities of contraceptive failure, pregnancy, unpreparedness for parenthood, and impairment of the wife's health. The Supreme Court ruled that Roe had standing to sue, but that the Does did not, ultimately dismissing their claim:

> Their claim is that, sometime in the future, Mrs. Doe might become pregnant because of possible failure of contraceptive measures, and, at that time in the future, she might want an abortion that might then be illegal under the Texas statutes.
>
> This very phrasing of the Does' position reveals its speculative character. Their alleged injury rests on possible future contraceptive failure, possible future pregnancy, possible future unpreparedness for parenthood, and possible future impairment of health. Any one or more of these several possibilities may not take place, and all may not combine. In the Does' estimation, these possibilities might have some real or imagined impact upon their marital happiness. But we are not prepared to say that the bare allegation of so indirect an injury is sufficient to present an actual case or controversy.[58]

It's important to note that Blackmun and the Court are criticizing the "speculative character" of this type of logic. The Does were basing their position on the *possibility* of something happening, its *likelihood*, and the Court dismissed this argument outright—and with good reason.

Yet Blackmun and the Court used this exact same logic as support for Roe in another part of the very same ruling, using this statement as part of their justification in section VIII:

> Maternity, or additional offspring, may force upon the woman a distressful life and future. Psychological harm may be imminent. Mental and physical health may be taxed by childcare. There is also the distress, for all concerned, associated with the unwanted child, and there is the problem of bringing a child into a family already unable, psychologically and otherwise, to care for it. In other cases, as in this one, the additional difficulties and continuing stigma of unwed motherhood may be involved.[59]

Their contradiction is obvious. Every statement hinges on a "may," which they now consider justification, despite the "or may not" inherent in every point. As the Court plainly states about the Does: "Any one or more of these several possibilities may not take place, and all may not combine." They conveniently forget this logic when they are arguing about Roe a few paragraphs later.

This reasoning—the Likelihood argument—continues to be presented as a justification for abortion. As the reasoning goes, it is better to prevent a birth than to bring children into homes where they are not wanted; or will suffer from illness, poverty, or disability; or may grow up to be criminals; or may impact the mother's health, happiness, or potential.

Of course, these things cannot be known—the child *may* be wanted the moment her mother holds her, *may* thrive and prosper despite less-than-ideal circumstances, and *may* improve the lives of all involved. Plenty of articles have been written about people throughout history (Einstein, Beethoven, etc.) who by all counts should have been aborted but beat the odds to change the world. The countless young mothers who were pressured to abort their babies but kept them and were later so thankful they did demonstrate that you can't accurately judge the likelihood of a life's impact, for better or worse.

This is the same nonsensical underlying philosophy that supports eugenics and population control, which we'll dive into more deeply later—the idea that "unwanted" babies, or babies born to poor families, or in less-than-ideal social conditions, or to certain races in certain places, or to single mothers, parents who don't want or didn't expect them, etc., etc., are *more likely* to negatively impact their parents, or society, or fail to be fulfilled adults themselves—and therefore taking their lives prebirth is justified.

The Likelihood argument is what I call the "God complex," in that we think we can determine the future potentiality of a person's life. That is, of course, nonsense, but it forces us to play God to make those determinations. Why do we have the hubris to think we can determine who is worthy to live and who is not based on what we think is the most probable end result?

But let's consider this from another angle. What if the soothsayers are correct? What if a child that could have been aborted *does* grow up to be a criminal? What if this person grows up and syphons money and resources from the system? What if the child negatively impacts the mother's well-being or opportunities?

If we are willing to kill humans before we even know if they will turn out to be criminals, poverty-stricken, or a disruption of the parents' lifestyle, why wouldn't we kill them when we *do* know that's how they have turned out? Why aren't abortion advocates in favor of killing off the thousands of prisoners in our justice system? Why aren't they recommending rounding up everyone below a certain income level and just euthanizing them? Certainly killing all criminals would be a very effective deterrent for the rest of us. Imagine all of the tax dollars that could be saved if we didn't have prisons. And it would save our government millions upon millions of dollars in aid and support if we just killed off the poor people that are currently benefiting from the system—to say nothing of the countless children who impact their parents' finances, education, or opportunities.

Does that sound inhumane? Of course it does. We would be considered barbarians, lunatics, and murderers if we sanctioned the killing of criminals, poor people, and 'inconvenient' children. We want the criminals to be reformed; we want to restore them to society. We want to implement programs and ministries to help poor people to lift themselves out of their depressed state. We want to aid and support struggling parents.

So, just to be clear, our current society sanctions the mass killing of preborn humans if they *might* turn out to be criminals, poor, or inconvenient. But if these humans have already turned out this way, then society has the obligation to preserve their lives and do what we can to assist them.

The logic is mystifying.

Now, we can't diminish the very real challenges that many parents face in difficult situations, and we should all acknowledge that these are real problems. On the surface, abortion helps certain struggling mothers out of tough circumstances. In a similar fashion, no-fault divorce does legitimately make it easier for women to escape abusive situations and domestic violence. Yet divorce leaves a trail of wreckage and similar familial results to abuse, exchanging one social ill for another. The answer isn't easier divorce—it's improving and empowering marriage and family.

In the same way, we can simultaneously work to solve these very real problems surrounding struggling mothers and still preserve life. As Dr. Randall O'Bannon writes:

> [A]bortion's legality and the implied social sanction that comes with it is clearly a major part of the cultural machinery that forces these cruel choices on women, that lets men off the hook, that leaves women to care for households of children all alone, and that makes society less accommodating to the demands of motherhood. Abortion forces on [women] a cruel, violent, destructive option that does little to solve their basic social or economic problems, problems, which may, in part, themselves be a consequence of Roe's forced cultural transformation. Those women would find better options and more respect for their rights and responsibilities as women and mothers with abortion off the table.[60]

We are smart enough as a society to address one problem without creating another. We can simultaneously focus on empowering women, improving conditions for impoverished peoples around the world, *and* supporting the rights of preborn humans. This position is not naïve or unrealistic; it is pragmatic and humanitarian. And unlike the Likelihood argument, it recognizes the worth and potential of all people.

Serrin Foster, president of Feminists for Life, writes:

> We insist on a world in which women have access to all nonviolent options. Think about the consequences of such a world for the workplace, schools, and society. We encourage woman-centered and parenting-friendly policies including distance learning, which allows a new mom to be with her child while continuing her education and saving on child-care costs; affordable family housing near campus; campus and workplace child care; health care plans for students and employees that include maternity coverage; telecommuting and job sharing; a living wage; and child support when one parent is absent. We have to approach this holistically.
>
> Pro-life feminists demand that society support the unique life-giving capacity of women, so that no woman feels driven to abortion. Women deserve better.[61]

"Meaningful Life": The Viability Argument

There is another reason that the *Roe v. Wade* ruling requires reexamination, one that is increasingly significant as time (and science) marches on. The Court's ruling pivots upon the concept of viability, or the point at which the baby can survive independent of the mother's body. The scope of individual states' powers to regulate (or even prohibit altogether) abortion depends upon this notion of viability. As the Court's ruling states in section X:

> With respect to the State's important and legitimate interest in potential life, the "compelling" point is at viability. This is so because the fetus then presumably has the capability of meaningful life outside the mother's womb. State regulation protective of fetal life after viability thus has both logical and biological justifications. If the State is interested in protecting fetal life after viability, it may go so far as to proscribe abortion during that period, except when it is necessary to preserve the life or health of the mother.[62]

A state's right to outlaw abortion during a set period of gestation—or put another way, the right to legalize the termination of the developing life—depends upon the ability of that life to survive outside the womb.

This is hugely problematic. We do not have value based on arbitrary criteria. We have value because of what we are. Yet the Supreme Court suggests we should define "meaningful life" (and when it should be legally protected) based on a changing scientific determination. As medical proficiency progresses, babies that were not viable forty years ago now clearly are. They can survive outside the womb at earlier and earlier ages of gestation. Should our determination of whether to protect a life be defined by our medical capabilities?

If we camp on this point for a moment, we see a very slippery slope evolving. If we do not determine value based on what we are (human beings), we can introduce all sorts of arbitrary criteria to determine our value. Viability is just one of a long list of variables that have been introduced to determine human value.

Size, age, location, degree of dependency, race, gender, circumstances of conception, medical condition, and several other criteria are already being used to determine whether or not a child lives or dies.

The baby isn't viable yet? Kill her. Disregard that viability has changed through the years and that plenty of born humans can't survive without direct intervention either.

The baby is really, really small? Kill him. Disregard the blatant discrimination. If a fetus is worth less than a newborn, then a toddler is worth less than a teenager because the toddler is smaller.

The baby is not yet twenty weeks in the womb? Kill her then. But if age is a factor in determining value, then a one-week-old newborn is worth less than a five-year-old. Why can't we kill the one-week-old?

The baby is dependent on the mother in the womb? We are free to kill him. Disregard the fact the same baby outside of the womb is also completely dependent on others to care for him.

The baby is African American? More than 50 percent of black babies in New York City are aborted,[63] so race selection must be OK.

The baby is a girl? Gender selection is part of many countries' standard fare, and it has already spread to America.

The baby was conceived as a result of rape or incest? Despite the fact the baby didn't commit the crime, the baby is the only party to receive the death penalty as a result. That's social justice for you.

The baby has the Zika virus or a cleft palate? Or Down Syndrome? We don't want medically challenged humans to drain our social system, so let's kill them (we abort over two-thirds of Down babies in America already).[64]

Any time we assign any variable to determine the value of preborn humans, other than the fact they are human, we discriminate against them. And by discriminating I don't mean sending them to the back of the bus or refusing to pick them for our dodgeball team. We kill them.

"The Case Collapses": The Personhood Argument

Thirdly, in an eerie echo of *Dred Scott*, *Roe* denied legal protection to the unborn because, as the Court concluded, "[T]he word 'person,' as used in the Fourteenth Amendment, does not include the unborn."[65] The Fourteenth Amendment was adopted in 1868 and declares, "No State shall . . . deprive any person of life, liberty, or property, without due process of law; nor deny to any person within its jurisdiction the equal protection of the laws."

The Court readily admitted that their arguments could not be supported if the developing child were determined to be a person, for then her rights would be protected:

> The appellee and certain *amici* argue that the fetus is a "person" within the language and meaning of the Fourteenth Amendment. In support of this, they outline at length and in detail the well known facts of fetal development. If this suggestion of personhood is established, the appellant's case, of course, collapses, for the fetus' right to life would then be guaranteed specifically by the Amendment.[66]

The Court asserted that personhood has strictly postnatal applications, distinguishing birth as the key event that grants personhood. Yet this contradicts both science and logic.

As numerous biologists have pointed out, birth, properly understood, is simply one step of human development, not the point at which human life begins:

"Although it is customary to divide human development into prenatal and postnatal periods, it is important to realize that birth is merely a dramatic event during development resulting in a change in environment."[67]

Logically, this only makes sense. If we are using the child's exit from the mother's womb as the defining factor of her personhood, this means her development is not the key criterion. A nonperson fetus in the womb Tuesday morning is suddenly a person Tuesday afternoon after birth. If labor is prolonged, that same child is in fact not a person Tuesday afternoon—is not subject to any of the protections of the Fourteenth Amendment—but is one Tuesday evening. If the doctor decides to induce labor Monday night, the child might attain personhood a whole day earlier. We are defining personhood based on timing and on a medical procedure, as if an individual suddenly attains this status because someone decides to make an incision or to facilitate labor.

In what other definitions is such logic accepted? Aside from a womb, is there any other location where an individual can gain or lose personhood if placed or removed? Is there any other medical procedure that grants or denies it?

Having determined that the unborn are not persons under the Fourteenth Amendment, the Court really didn't have to opine on when life begins. Blackmun punted, claiming that since "those trained in the respective disciplines of medicine, philosophy, and theology are unable to arrive at any consensus [about when life begins], the judiciary, at this point in the development of man's knowledge, is not in a position to speculate as to the answer." [68]

When life begins is no deep conundrum at all. And it's not a theological or philosophical question. We're not asking who the author of life is or what rules He has ordained for the living. Nor are we asking what the value or purpose of life is. When we ask *when* life begins, we're asking a scientific question that science can answer. And it has done so definitively. Life begins at conception, i.e., fertilization. As Dr. Alfred M. Bongioanni, professor of pediatrics and obstetrics at the University of Pennsylvania, stated before a US Senate judiciary subcommittee: "I submit that human life is present throughout this entire sequence from conception to adulthood. . . . I am no more prepared to say that these early stages [of development in the womb] represent an incomplete human being than I would be to say that the child prior to the dramatic effects of puberty . . . is not a human being. This is human life at every stage."[69]

Or Professor Hymie Gordon, Mayo Clinic: "By all the criteria of modern molecular biology, life is present at the moment of conception."[70]

Or Professor Micheline Matthews-Roth, Harvard University Medical School: "It is scientifically correct to say that an individual human life begins at conception."[71]

The Official Senate report on Senate Bill 158 summed it up in this way: "Physicians, biologists, and other scientists agree that conception marks the beginning of the life of a human being—a being that is alive and is a member of the human species. There is overwhelming agreement on this point in countless medical, biological, and scientific writings."[72]

But *Roe* does not cite science. It simply says the unborn are not persons in the eyes of the law, just as African American slaves were not persons under the *Dred Scott* decision. As horrific as slavery was, the "liberty" granted in *Roe* is much worse, since it grants a freedom not merely to own and enslave other humans—but to use deadly force against weak and vulnerable members of the human family.

The Court stated, "We need not resolve the difficult question of when life begins." Oddly, they seemingly take a pass on this "question of when life begins," which is not difficult at all and has been scientifically established for decades, yet they are comfortable defining "meaningful life"—which would appear a much trickier proposition.

Similarly, in their 1992 ruling in *Planned Parenthood v. Casey*, the Court opined: "At the heart of liberty is the right to define one's own concept of existence, of meaning of the universe, and the mystery of human life."[73] As Timothy Keller points out, "The statement does not say we are free to 'discover' truth for ourselves but rather to 'define' it ourselves—including 'the mystery of human life.' Yet, by denying personhood, they are taking it upon themselves to define human life, depriving this right of liberty to all others—most specifically the unborn."[74]

Even were we to ignore the inconsistencies in their arguments and grant the Supreme Court the right to determine when "meaningful life" occurs and to define "personhood" based on a set of criteria, there are many, many reasons the Court should have granted personhood to the unborn—whether or not it was "in accord with the results" of previous cases or prevailing notions of personhood "throughout the major portion of the 19th century," as Blackmun noted.[75] After all, the unborn weren't the only ones being denied personhood throughout much of the 1800s.

Alcorn, in his excellent book *ProLife Answers to ProChoice Arguments*, includes many points relevant to the question of personhood:

A body part is defined by the common genetic code it shares with the rest of its body; the unborn's genetic code differs from his mother's.

The child may die and the mother live, or the mother may die and the child live, proving they are two separate individuals.

The unborn child takes an active role in his own development, controlling the course of the pregnancy and the time of birth.

Being inside something is not the same as being part of something.

Human beings should not be discriminated against because of their place of residence.

Like *toddler* and *adolescent*, the terms *embryo* and *fetus* do not refer to nonhumans, but to humans at particular stages of development.

Prior to the earliest abortions, the unborn already has every body part she will ever have.

Every abortion stops a beating heart and terminates measurable brain waves.

Even in the earliest surgical abortions, the unborn child is clearly human in appearance.

Even before the unborn is obviously human in appearance, she is what she is—a human being.

The ovum and sperm are each a product of another's body; unlike the conceptus, neither is an independent entity.

Something nonhuman does not become human by getting older and bigger; whatever is human must be human from the beginning.

Personhood is properly defined by membership in the human species, not by stage of development within that species.

Personhood is not a matter of size, skill, or degree of intelligence.

The unborn's status should be determined on an objective basis, not on subjective or self-serving definitions of personhood.

It is a scientific fact that there are thought processes at work in unborn babies.

There is nothing about birth that makes a baby essentially different than he was before birth.

Once we grant that the unborn are human beings, it should settle the question of their right to live.[76]

There is no gauge of personhood that denies the status to the unborn—location, intelligence, self-awareness, ability to survive unassisted, age, size, or any other—that, if applied to all humans, would not make some born people "lesser" persons. Children, the elderly, those with disabilities or certain medical conditions, and countless others would have to be considered lower on the scale of personhood, without full claim to their Constitutional rights.

As Randy Alcorn has stated, "It is dangerous when people in power are free to determine whether other, less powerful lives are meaningful."[77]

The Court's ruling in *Roe v. Wade* should be recognized for what it was—in error, riddled with inconsistent and arbitrary reasoning, and an overstepping of the Court's responsibility to adhere to the Constitution's provisions. As stated by Supreme Court Justice Byron White, who dissented in *Roe v. Wade* and critiqued the *Roe* decision in the Court's dissent for *Doe v. Bolton*:

> I find nothing in the language or history of the Constitution to support the Court's judgment. The Court simply fashions and announces a new constitutional right for pregnant mothers and, with scarcely any reason or authority for its action, invests that right with sufficient substance to override most existing state abortion statutes. . . . As an exercise of raw judicial power, the Court perhaps has authority to do what it does today; but, in my view, its judgment is an improvident and extravagant exercise of the power of judicial review that the Constitution extends to this court.[78]

Justice White expanded on his position thirteen years later in his dissent in *Thornburgh v. American College of Obstetricians and Gynecologists*:

> When the Court ventures further and defines as "fundamental" liberties that are nowhere mentioned in the Constitution . . . it must, of necessity, act with more caution, lest it open itself to the accusation that, in the name of identifying constitutional principles to which the people have consented in framing their Constitution, the Court has done nothing more than impose its own controversial choices of value upon the people. . . . I would return the issue to the people by overruling *Roe v. Wade*.[79]

The flaws in the Likelihood, Viability, and Personhood arguments, and others, should cause us to seriously examine the Supreme Court's ruling on abortion.

Slavery was legal because the law determined African Americans were not persons.

Abortion is legal because the law determined preborn humans are not persons.

Was slavery legal? Yes. Was it good? No.

Is abortion legal? Yes. Is it good?

The fact that abortion is legal, freely practiced, and socially acceptable does not mean it is good for women. It just means it is legal, freely practiced, and socially acceptable.

Slavery met the same criteria, though today we consider slavery to be reprehensible, noting that the practice is inherently discriminatory toward slaves. And, if you think about it, abortion is equally discriminatory against a whole class of human beings—those who are small, dependent, voiceless, and in a location where we can't see them without medical assistance.

Is She a Person or Not?

Then there are those circumstances that call the legality of abortion into question altogether.

On April 13, 2003, the body of a late-term male fetus washed up on the shore of San Francisco Bay. One day later, the partial body of his mother washed up a mile or so away.

Though the exact cause of death was never determined, it was concluded that the mother, Laci Peterson, was murdered by her husband, Scott.

Scott was charged and convicted of first-degree murder in the death of his wife.

He was also charged with second-degree murder in the death of his unborn son, Conner.

The situation is tragic, sad—and incredibly ironic. Scott was charged with second-degree murder in the death of his unborn son, yet, in many states, Laci could have aborted the same child, and it would have been perfectly legal.

So Conner's death was illegal because his dad caused it, but it would have been perfectly legal if his mom had caused it.

This high-profile crime led to a federal law that defies logic—the Unborn Victims of Violence Act.

Signed into law in 2004 by President George W. Bush, "Laci and Conner's Law" recognizes a child *in utero* as a legal victim if he or she is injured or killed during the act of over sixty federal crimes of violence. The law defines the unborn child as a member of the species *Homo sapiens*, at any stage of development, who is carried in the mother's womb.

The law has a specific exemption for abortion that didn't satisfy its critics. Senator John Kerry voted against the bill, remarking, "I have serious concerns about this legislation because the law cannot simultaneously provide that a fetus is a human being and protect the right of the mother to choose to terminate her pregnancy."[80]

Senator Kerry made a valid point. One law protects the unborn child at any stage of development from acts of violence, yet another law denies the same protection to the same child. Apparently the value and status of the child is determined by who does the act of violence—not the child itself. One law makes it clear that the unborn child is a member of the human race, while the other isn't sure but allows for the willful termination of the life anyhow.

There are now thirty-eight states with fetal-homicide laws that criminalize causing the death of an unborn child; twenty-three of these

48

have statutes that apply to any stage of pregnancy. At least fifteen have laws that make the pregnancy of a homicide victim an aggravating factor that can lead to the death penalty. In almost every state, women have been arrested or detained for exposing their fetuses to illegal drugs; in more than half of them, mothers can lose custody rights if they or their newborn tests positive for controlled substances.[81]

Women can be penalized for harming their babies, but not for killing them. It is a crime for a father to end the life of his pregnant wife's child, but the mother can do it without breaking any law. A woman can be convicted for killing another's unborn child, but not her own. The inconsistency is plainly apparent and abhorrent.

In Judge Tom Parker's main opinion in 2013's *Ex Parte Ankron and Kimbrough* for the Alabama Supreme Court, he cited "laws that give inheritance rights to unborn children, laws that ban pregnant inmates from being executed, laws that give fetuses legal guardians for the purposes of protecting their interests, laws that allow parents to sue for damages if fetuses are injured or killed as the result of negligence or some other wrongful act." Parker compiled lists of statutes from around the United States that confer fetal rights, and he concluded, "Today, the only major area in which unborn children are denied legal protection is abortion, and that denial is only because of the dictates of *Roe*."[82]

Laci and Conner's Law, other fetal-homicide laws, and the ruling of *Roe v. Wade* are all legal—while completely paradoxical. And, in the worst form of discrimination, the value of the human life in the womb is determined, legally, by whoever opts to take that life.

So we must, therefore, look at abortion through a different lens for two reasons. Current US law regarding the status of the unborn is in conflict with itself, and just because something is legal doesn't make it right or good.

Likewise, the fact that we say abortion is about women's rights does not mean it advances gender equality.

Just as it is vital to remind ourselves about the racial and selfish reasons behind slavery, we must also peer behind the curtain to understand the rationale behind the legality of abortion.

So, yes, abortion is legal. But that doesn't mean it is automatically good for women, families, and society as a whole.

PART 1
Men Started It

CHAPTER 3
A Long History of Men Behaving Badly

While there are millions of examples of wise, kind, gentle, and respectful men in history, there are also far too many examples of men who took it upon themselves to treat women as property.

Men often actively seek to use women to their own ends. And sometimes men accomplish the same ends by doing nothing.

Abortion is, indeed, about protecting women's rights, but not in the way that our current culture thinks. A review of the past and present injustices visited upon women by men will provide some context and allow us to better understand abortion in the light of men persecuting women.

Ancient Men Behaving Badly

The most famous example of a man standing by while his wife hurt herself happened in an ancient and beautiful garden. Though Adam was with his perfect wife, Eve, in the Garden of Eden when she fatefully took a bite of the forbidden fruit, he still managed to blame God when he went right along with her disobedience.

When God inquired what had happened, Adam replied, "The woman whom You gave *to be* with me, she gave me of the tree, and I ate" (Genesis

3:12). Not only did Adam sit by when Eve was tempted to disobey, but he refused to take responsibility for not protecting his own wife.

After Adam and Eve were cast out of the garden, things went downhill for women in general. Most ancient civilizations viewed women as slaves and property.

In ancient Greece, women had little to no freedom. Historian and biographer Plutarch remarked that women were to be kept "under lock and key." In a play by Aristophanes, the female character, Calonice, says, "We women can't go out just when we like. We have to wait upon our men."[83]

Sociologist Alvin J. Schmidt gives a troubling overview of the way women were treated in ancient Greece. Schmidt, author of *How Christianity Changed the World*, details the ways in which the average woman had the social status of a slave:

She had no legal ability to divorce her husband.

Girls were not allowed to attend school and receive an education.

Women were not allowed to speak in public.

Legally, women were deemed to be inferior to men.

Infanticide was common, and the babies killed were overwhelmingly female.

Ancient Rome treated women much the same. At the time of Christ, according to Schmidt, women had "none of the rights and privileges that men enjoyed."

Husbands had absolute control of wives and their possessions. Women owned nothing.

Wives could not divorce their husbands.

Women could not inherit property.

The law gave a husband the right to physically punish his wife. That punishment could include death.

Women were not allowed to speak in public.[84]

The relative worth of girls in the ancient world is revealed in this astonishing first-century letter from a Roman man to his pregnant wife:

> I send you my warmest greetings. I want you to know that we are still in Alexandria. And please don't worry. . . . If you have the baby before I return, if it is a boy, let it live; if it is a girl expose it. . . .[85]

Sexually, women were tools for men's pleasure. Church historian Philip Schaff remarks, "The virtue of chastity, in our Christian sense, was almost unknown among the heathens. Woman was essentially a slave of man's lower passions."[86]

Plutarch notes that child brides were common, with girls being married off as young as twelve. These girls had no options, no choices, and no voice about who they married.

Women were also held in low regard in first-century Jewish culture. The Talmud, for example, contains this observation: "The world cannot exist without males and without females—happy is he whose children are males, and woe to him whose children are females."[87] The testimony of women was regarded as suspect or not accepted. As first-century Jewish historian Josephus wrote, "But let not the testimony of women be admitted, on account of the levity and boldness of their sex. . . ."[88]

Until Christianity worked to stop the practice in Hindu India, the burning of widows was a common occurrence. It was considered the duty of a good wife to sacrifice herself on her husband's funeral pyre. According to a Hindu saying, "If her husband is happy, she should be happy; if he is sad, she should be sad; and if he is dead, she should also die."[89] This duty was forcibly imposed on willing and unwilling widows. The practice was also common in pre-Christian Scandinavia, China, New Zealand, and among some American Indians, prior to Columbus's arrival.[90]

In China, binding women's feet was common practice for centuries. The process, involving painfully and tightly wrapping young girls' feet to prevent normal growth, often resulted in lifelong disability, pain, and lack of mobility for the women. Why did Chinese men institute and promote foot binding? Because they found women with a limited gait more attractive.[91]

Though it can be argued that men have found numerous ways to mistreat, torture, and abuse other men (slavery, for instance), there are no national examples of women binding men's feet, forcing them to wear certain articles of clothing, using them as property for their own pleasure, or having the legal right to kill their husbands.

In the interaction of genders across world history, if inequality and abuse was present, it was always women suffering at the hands of men.

Female inequality, exploitation, and maltreatment are not limited to ancient times in other cultures. America, too, has a long history of female inequality.

American Men Behaving Badly

Not that women in early America experienced anything like the oppression and mistreatment of women in the ancient world. Women in America have historically enjoyed far more freedom than in any other culture. In *Democracy in America*, Alexis de Tocqueville's epic survey of 1830s America, the author remarks, "[W]omen of the United States are confined within the narrow circle of domestic life, and their situation is in some respects one of extreme dependence." At the same time, "I have nowhere seen women occupying a loftier position."[92]

Yet women in nineteenth-century America did not have equal rights with men. They did not have the right to vote, lost property rights when they married, and had few options for divorce or employment outside the home. As the Declaration of Sentiments, a feminist document signed at the 1856 Seneca Falls Convention, put it, speaking of the male-dominant society at the time:

> He has never permitted her to exercise her inalienable right to the elective franchise.
>
> He has compelled her to submit to laws, in the formation of which she had no voice.
>
> He has withheld from her rights which are given to the most ignorant and degraded men—both natives and foreigners.
>
> Having deprived her of this first right of a citizen, the elective franchise, thereby leaving her without representation in the halls of legislation, he has oppressed her on all sides.[93]

It was not until 1920 that American women won the right to vote with the passage of the Nineteenth Amendment. The first thirty-three American presidents were men elected by men (though some states permitted women to vote in 1916). And though the 1940s saw women joining the armed forces and entering the labor force in new ways due to World War II, their narrowly circumscribed social role returned in the 1950s, limiting access to education, jobs, and any opportunities outside of running the home and raising a family.

And while America has arguably been the most progressive country in moving toward equal rights for women, many parts of the world are still in the dark ages of gender inequality.

Modern Men Behaving Badly

I had lunch with a new friend who works in the medical field in the African country of Uganda. I asked him about the culture, the medical facilities, and the presence of abortion. My friend, Emma (a man's name in his country), told me abortion is illegal in Uganda, though widely practiced. When I asked him how that could be, he replied, "The women do the work. They bear the children, raise the children, and also have to work to provide for their families. So they get abortions because they have no money and no help around the home."

"What do the men do?" I asked.

"Nothing. They sit around all day. They drink and smoke."

"They do nothing?" I inquired with surprise.

"Nothing. Lazy. They think women should do everything."

Although many Ugandan men may not fit this mold, it reveals a troubling societal pattern. This chauvinistic philosophy and practice is not limited to Uganda. It is widely reported in numerous African countries—and many would see in it an extreme parallel to the countless women in America (and around the world) left by their husbands to fend for themselves and their families.

In the Middle East, Sharia law is used in many Islamic nations to impose strict and restrictive laws on women. In Saudi Arabia, the birthplace of Islam, the law places severe limitations on women. Under Saudi law and custom, for example, women:

are not allowed to go out without male accompaniment,

are not allowed to drive,

are not allowed to vote, and

must, in most cases, wear a head covering, a full black cloak, and a face veil when out in public.

"Saudi society is based on enslavement—the enslavement of women to men and of society to the state," Wajiha Al-Huweidar, a Saudi Arabian woman and activist for women's rights, said on Al-Hurra TV on January 13, 2008. "People still do not make their own decisions," she said, "but it is the women of Saudi Arabia who have been denied everything. The Saudi woman still lives the life of a slave girl."[94]

Other Islamic nations, including Egypt, impose strict regulations on female movement and lifestyle. Egyptian-born Noni Darwish noted the practical implications of such restrictions. In her book *Cruel and Usual Punishment*, which reveals the harsh impact of Sharia law on women, Darwish writes, "For the first thirty years of my life, I lived as a virtual slave. I was a bird in a cage: a second-class citizen who had to watch what I said even to my close friends."[95]

Darwish, born in 1949, writes, "During my years in Egypt, the vast majority of Muslim women lived in cramped apartments or unhealthy little mud huts, spending their entire lives working hard under the severe Egyptian sun."

There are numerous examples of Muslim women publicly executed because they were raped or suspected of adultery. In Bangladesh, a fourteen-year-old girl collapsed and died after receiving seventy lashes. Her punishment came after an older male cousin allegedly attacked, gagged, and raped her. A local imam said she was guilty of adultery and sentenced her to a public whipping of one hundred lashes. CNN reported that her parents "watched as the whip broke the skin of their youngest child and she fell unconscious to the ground."[96]

The brutality is even more horrific in Iran. A member of the Basiji militia, an Iranian paramilitary group, told a *Jerusalem Post* reporter that prison officials in Iran subject young women to rape prior to their executions. It's all perfectly legal. Islamic law prohibits the execution of virgins, so unmarried women sentenced to die are married off to prison guards, followed by their legalized rape. After that cruel crime is committed against them, they are executed.

"I remember hearing them cry and scream after [the rape] was over," the Basiji militia member said. "I will never forget how this one girl clawed at her own face and neck with her fingernails afterwards. She had deep scratches all over her."[97]

And America is not immune from Islamic oppression of women. Sixteen-year-old Christian convert Rifqa Bary ran away from her home in Ohio in 2009. She fled for fear that her Muslim father would carry out an "honor killing" against her because she had left Islam. "He would kill me or send me back to Sri Lanka," she said after arriving in Florida. A custody fight ensued, and Rifqa's Sri Lankan parents' effort to force her to return home failed after she turned eighteen and obtained permanent residency status in the United States.[98]

Rifqa's claim that she would be killed was not unfounded. Other Muslim girls have been killed in the United States for adopting Western ways or acting immodestly in the view of their parents. The father of twenty-year-old Noor Almaleki ran her over with a car, leaving Noor with severe injuries from which she died. A police investigator said Noor "was run down in broad daylight by her father who was angry that she had become too Westernized and did not want to accept a marriage her father had arranged for her in the family's native Iraq."[99]

In Iraq, women have faced rising levels of sectarian violence in recent years, resulting in a plummeting literacy rate—though once the highest in the Arab world—as families fear their daughters will be kidnapped or raped if sent to school. As the *Guardian* reported in 2007, there have been times that hospitals have flooded with dead women with no one willing to identify their cause of death;

if someone came to claim a body, she was said to have had an "accident." Women may encounter abuse or abduction if they do not wear a *hijab*, the traditional Muslim head scarf, and face the risks of trafficking and sexual slavery, after which they may be treated like criminals themselves and face further abuse while in detention. Honor killings and murder rates of women have both been rising. Beyond efforts to gain equal rights, many women are struggling for the very right to live.[100]

Around the world, in country after country, women continue to face oppression in a variety of forms that cripple their hopes, limit their opportunities, and subject them to violence and discrimination.

"These things are universal," says Taina Bien-Aime, executive director of New York–based Equality Now. "There is not one single country where women can feel absolutely safe."[101]

In Afghanistan, the average female life expectancy is only forty-five years, one year less than for an Afghan male. An overwhelming number of women are illiterate, more than half of all brides are under the age of sixteen, and one woman dies in childbirth every hour. Domestic violence runs rampant; nearly nine out of every ten women admit experiencing it. More than one million widows live on the streets, often forced into prostitution. Afghanistan is the only country in the world with a higher suicide rate for women than for men.

In Nepal, widows experience extreme abuse and discrimination if someone in the community labels them *bokshi*, meaning witches. Daughters who are not married off are often sold to traffickers before they even reach their teens.

Guatemala is home to an impoverished underclass of women who face domestic violence, rape, and the second-highest rate of HIV/AIDS after sub-Saharan Africa. The country has seen an epidemic of vicious, unsolved murders that has killed hundreds of women, some of their bodies mutilated and marked with hate messages.

One of the globe's poorest countries, Mali, sees many girls forced into early marriage, and few escape the torture of genital mutilation. One in ten women dies in pregnancy or childbirth.[102]

In December 2012, the *New York Times* reported on the decades-long conflict that has ravaged the Democratic Republic of Congo, where "it is as if the real battlefields are women's bodies":

> Out here, hundreds of thousands of women have been systematically assaulted in recent years, leading the United Nations to call Congo "the rape capital of the world." Many of these rapes have been marked by a level of brutality that is shocking even by the twisted standards of a place rived by civil war and haunted by warlords and drugged-up child soldiers. What's the strategic purpose of putting an AK-47 assault rifle inside a woman and pulling the trigger? Or cutting out a woman's fetus and making her friends eat it?[103]

These rapes have become so brutal and widespread that UN investigators called them "unprecedented." Many of the victims die; others are infected with HIV and cast aside to care for children alone. They must forage for food and water, which exposes them to still more violence. They have no options for safety, protection, or escape.[104]

In the currently ongoing civil war in South Sudan, a new UN report recently revealed that soldiers have been allowed to rape and enslave women in lieu of collecting their salaries. Not only are women not spared by the fighting, but they are "targeted by soldiers who use sexual violence as a tool of oppression and even a form of combat pay." In just one of the ten states making up this nation, there were over 1,300 reported cases of sexual violence in a five-month period. Girls as young as five were raped.

"This is one of the most horrendous human-rights situations in the world, with massive use of rape as an instrument of terror and weapon of war," said UN High Commissioner for Human Rights Zeid Ra`ad Al Hussein.[105]

The stories of oppression and violence continue in community after community, nation after nation.

Even in wealthier countries, women may face repressive laws, enforced ignorance, and systemic oppression. In other countries, often those that are poorest and facing internal conflict, women face extreme degrees of violence on a daily basis. Refugee women are frequently among the most vulnerable. Human rights groups have identified countries where violations against women are so severe that even murder is routine.

"While the potential of women is recognized at the international level," says World Health Organization director-general Margaret Chan, "this potential will not be realized until conditions improve—often dramatically—in countries and communities."[106]

A few additional facts:

Women make up 80 percent of all refugees and displaced people.[107]

As of January 2012, women held only 15.1 percent of all presiding officer posts in governments of the world.[108]

Over 60 million girls worldwide are child brides, married before the age of eighteen.[109]

603 million women live in countries where domestic violence is not yet considered a crime.[110]

World history and modern culture suggest that we are far, far away from true gender equality. Every major historical incident of one gender being persecuted by another is a case of women being persecuted by men.

This disheartening world tour is beginning to form a picture of the culture we live in, the context for the life-and-death decisions men and women make on a daily basis, including abortion. There are other, equally disturbing aspects that we must consider to reach a full understanding, though, and many of them hit very, very close to home.

CHAPTER 4
Objectified in America

Women around the world face violence and oppression, and they are often particularly vulnerable due to the political climate, cultural environment, or economic factors. In many countries, they earn less than men, have a smaller voice in government, and suffer from limited opportunities for education and advancement. Their enfranchisement and empowerment are stymied at every turn, and repression often takes even more brutal, bloody, and sinister forms.

In perhaps its most disturbing iterations, the oppression of women revolves around sexual abuse and exploitation. Rape, as the first example, is not only a major problem in war-torn countries—it is a threat faced all too often by women in the United States, as well.

Rape in the United States

According to the US Department of Justice's National Crime Victimization Survey, there is an average of 293,066 victims (age twelve or older) of rape and sexual assault each year.[111] This means that every 107 seconds, another American is sexually assaulted.

Although males are undeniably victims of sexual assault as well and deserve the same support and intervention, by far the majority of victims are female and offenders are male. According to the FBI, in 2012 there were over 67,000 female sex offense victims and 12,000 male victims; that same year, male convicted sex offenders numbered 78,500 and female offenders 4,394.[112]

Rape prevalence among women in the United States (the percentage of women who experienced rape at least once in their lifetime so far) is in the range of 15–20 percent, with different studies disagreeing with each other. This means one out of every five to six women has been the victim of an attempted or completed rape.[113]

Studies have shown that sexual assaults are grossly underreported in the United States, with the majority of assaults going unreported to the police (an average of 68 percent of assaults in the last five years were not reported).[114] Additionally, a 2014 research paper comparing correlations in murder and rape rates determined that police departments in about 22 percent of the 210 American cities examined in the study eliminate or undercount rapes from official records in part to "create the illusion of success in fighting violent crime."[115]

Even when the crime is reported and documented, it is unlikely to lead to an arrest and prosecution. Factoring in unreported rapes, only about 2 percent of rapists will ever serve a day in prison. The other 98 percent walk away free.[116]

Trafficking and Slavery

Human trafficking and modern-day slavery remain major human-rights concerns around the world that once again disproportionately target and affect women. The International Labour Organization estimates that there are 20.9 million victims of human trafficking globally, and the US Department of Labor has identified 136 goods from seventy-four countries made by forced and child labor.[117]

In 2012, the United Nations held a special General Assembly meeting in which top officials urged member states "to increase their collaborative efforts to prevent human trafficking and protect its victims." The UN Office on Drugs and Crime reported that the crime of human trafficking generates $32 billion annually—an amount rivaling the profits gained by the illicit trade in arms and drugs. The UN reported that women comprise two-thirds of trafficking victims.[118]

According to the 2014 Global Slavery Index, a report released by the Walk Free Foundation, 35.8 million people around the world are estimated to live in slavery.[119]

Though we may be tempted to think of the United States as a bastion of freedom and security, this nation is by no means a safe refuge for girls and women being trafficked. The United States serves as a major transit and destination country for human trafficking. An estimated 14,500 to 17,500 people, primarily women and children, are trafficked to the United States annually for purposes of forced labor or sexual exploitation.[120]

According to the Polaris Project, a nonprofit organization that works to combat modern-day slavery and trafficking:

In 2014, an estimated one out of six endangered runaways reported to the National Center for Missing and Exploited Children was likely a child sex-trafficking victim. Of those, 68 percent were in the care of social services or foster care when they ran.[121]

The Super Bowl is the single-largest incident of human trafficking in the United States. As hundreds of thousands of fans converge upon the Super Bowl host city, it becomes an optimal breeding ground for forced workers, Texas Attorney General Greg Abbott told *USA Today* back in 2011. Sex-trafficking victims are brought to the host city to work, and one survivor told the *Times-Picayune* that she was expected to sleep with around twenty-five men a day during such events.[122]

Pornography: An American Obsession

Then there is pornography. It's almost ubiquitous in American culture. It is the most viewed subject online, according to *Time* magazine writer Pamela Paul, who reports that "66% of 18–34-year-old men visit a pornographic site every month."[58] The effects are altogether negative. Porn teaches men to regard women as sex objects and lowers the threshold to violence against women. So-called "adult entertainment" is linked to:

Seeing women as sex toys: A 2009 study used MRI scans of men who viewed pornography to conclude that porn viewing led men to see women as sexual objects.[123]

Divorce and infidelity: Those who have seen an X-rated movie in the last year are "25.6% more likely to be divorced, 65.1% more likely to report having had an extramarital affair, [and] 8.0% less likely to report having a 'very happy' marriage (if they are still married). . . ."[124]

Addiction and its fallout: When viewing pornography becomes an addiction, 40 percent of addicts lose their spouses, 58 percent suffer considerable financial losses, and about a third lose their jobs.[125]

Sexual violence: A survey of college men at a midwestern university found that "men who view pornography are significantly less likely to intervene as a bystander, report an increased behavioral intent to rape, and are more likely to believe rape myths."[126] Executed serial killer Ted Bundy, who murdered at least twenty-eight women, said his sadistic behavior found its origin in his addiction to hardcore pornography. One of Bundy's last victims was a twelve-year-old girl, whose body he dumped in a pigsty.[127] Studies have shown that individuals who were convicted of the collection and distribution of internet child pornography had also committed, on average, over thirteen different child sex abuses.[128]

To make matters worse, you support trafficking when you watch porn. Even if a pornographic video claims that all actors are over eighteen and have given their consent to be filmed, it may not be true; the trafficked actresses may have been trained to look and act older.[129]

As the *Huffington Post* reported in 2014, "the implication of the porn industry is human sex trafficking and bondage." Human sex trafficking has been repeatedly linked to prostitution, which is then linked to pornography.[130] Individuals become trapped or forced into sex and become the subjects for pornographic videos and pictures for others' viewing pleasure, a vicious cycle of abuse with no escape. Those are real people behind the pictures, and that is real suffering making it possible.

Fight the New Drug is a movement that advocates ending pornography and puts the connection succinctly: "In the end, porn fuels prostitution; and porn and prostitution are the products the sex trade exists to deliver," their website states.

Whether illicit images, an escort service, a lap dance from a stripper, or a visit with a prostitute, the sex industry exists to meet self-serving desire and indulgent pleasure, which invariably depend on the exploitation of others. It is a process of dehumanizing women that pervades this industry, including both the production and consumption of pornography—and it is only getting worse.

Extreme and Violent

In 2010, the *Guardian* ran an article on activist and academic Gail Dines, author of *Pornland: How Porn Has Hijacked Our Sexuality.*[131] Although pornography is more widely accepted than ever, it has moved far beyond mild titillation and mere nudity into alarmingly high demand for extreme and violent acts. "We are now bringing up a generation of boys on cruel, violent porn," Dines says, "and given what we know about how images affect people, this is going to have a profound influence on their sexuality, behavior and attitudes towards women."

According to Dines's research, technological shifts supplying a readily accessible stream of porn mean that men are becoming desensitized to it and are therefore seeking out increasingly harsh, violent, and degrading images—such that even the porn industry is shocked, with industry conferences discussing the growing trend for extreme acts. Acts and images that were nearly nonexistent a decade ago, due to their brutality or extremism, have now become commonplace. The audience is also getting younger; market research found that the average age a boy first sees porn today is eleven.

"I have found that the earlier men use porn," says Dines, "the more likely they are to have trouble developing close, intimate relationships with real women. . . . They are bewildered, even angry, when real women don't want or enjoy porn sex."

Pornography also changes the ways that women and girls think about their bodies, sexuality, and relationships, according to Dines. "Every group that has fought for liberation understands that media images are part and parcel of the systematic dehumanization of an oppressed group. . . . The more porn images filter into mainstream culture, the more girls and women are stripped of full human status and reduced to sex objects."

Dines observes, "Many on the liberal left adopt a view that says pornographers are not businessmen but are simply there to unleash our sexuality from state-imposed constraints." This view was reflected in the film *The People vs. Larry Flynt*, where the billionaire pornographer of the film's title—the head of the Hustler empire—was portrayed as a man simply fighting for freedom of speech. Similarly, Hugh Hefner has stated, "I've always felt I was on the side of the angels," and he proudly told *Esquire*, "I was a feminist before there was such a thing as feminism."[132]

Dines would contest this view that pornographers are driven by any such ennobling goals. "Trust me," she says, "I have interviewed hundreds of pornographers, and the only thing that gets them excited is profit."

Ironically, the public has become so desensitized to nudity that now even *Playboy* no longer considers it a novelty; the magazine has recently made the decision to no longer feature fully nude photos.

The prevalence of pornography in our culture is doing more, though, than desensitizing. As the *Guardian* reports, Dines's research leads her to believe that pornography is driving men to commit particular acts of violence toward women. "I am not saying that a man reads porn and goes out to rape," she says, "but what I do know is that porn gives permission to its consumers to treat women as they are treated in porn." Recent studies and reports from sexual-assault centers at US colleges confirm her belief, noting the rising incidence of sexual acts common in extreme pornography.

"The more porn sexualizes violence against women, the more it normalizes and legitimizes sexually abusive behavior," Dines says. "Men learn about sex from porn, and in porn nothing is too painful or degrading for women." Her research also notes the rising popularity of what she calls "childified porn," with almost 14 million Internet searches for "teen sex" in 2006, an increase of more than 60 percent since 2004. Dines's research shows that regular exposure to such material breaks down the taboo of having sex with children, and her interviews with numerous convicted child rapists showed that all were habitual users of child pornography who were initially horrified by the thought before exposing themselves to these images.

Dines has faced fierce criticism from the industry and from pro-porn activists, and her college receives letters after any public event at which she is speaking, attacking her views. "The assumption that if you are a woman who hates pornography you are against sex shows how successful the industry is at collapsing porn into sex." Yet Dines believes that the threat to women and to our culture requires a united campaign to defeat it, one that cannot be discouraged or deterred in spite of opposition. "What is at stake is the nature of the world that we live in," she says. "We have to wrestle it back."

Stories of Exploitation

Numerous women have come forward to share their stories of being exploited as part of the porn industry, from Rashida Jones's documentary *Hot Girls Wanted* to Holly Madison's book *Down the Rabbit Hole*, which describes her life in the Playboy mansion, where she lived as Hugh Hefner's girlfriend. Their stories reflect the examples of "countless other women who have been involved in the sex industry—unjust distribution of income, tight leashes, deceit and manipulation, and unwanted sexual relations, among others."[133] The industry suffers from rampant manipulation and very little regulation. Subsequent risks and abuses abound, ranging from physical abuse to common sexually transmitted diseases and AIDS. Women often enter the industry out of dire financial need and limited options, only to get caught in the system and fail to make enough to escape it—despite the staggering amount of profits it generates.

According to research conducted by Debby Herbenick and Bryant Paul of the Kinsey Institute for *Hot Girls Wanted*, more people visit porn sites each month than Netflix, Amazon, and Twitter combined. The porn industry overall makes more than $13 billion in profit every year. For context, that's more than Hollywood, which makes around $8 billion. That's also more than Microsoft, Google, Amazon, eBay, Yahoo, and Apple combined. Despite all this money, and despite women being the main commodity, men are usually in charge and are taking the lion's share of the profit as they control the women. The stories of women who have come forward demonstrate the prevalence of pimping and trafficking of women in the porn industry, as well as widespread abuse and rape. As painful, shocking, violent acts become increasingly commonplace in pornography, more and more women are coerced into enduring them, even if they were not part of the original agreement.

According to Herbenick and Paul's research, in 2014, abuse porn websites averaged over 60 million combined hits per month—more hits than NFL.com, NBA.com, Hotwire.com, CBS.com, Fortune.com, Disney.com, and NBCNews.com. Other researchers found that over 88 percent of top-rated porn scenes contain aggressive acts, and 94 percent of the time, the violence is directed toward a woman.[134]

Studies have shown that exposure to even nonviolent sexual acts increases levels of aggression in viewers[135] and that exposure to violent sexual acts triggers even higher levels of aggression.[136]

A review of meta-analyses (Allen, D'Alessio, & Brezgel, 1995) and single studies (Baron & Straus, 1987; Fisher & Barak, 1991; Garcia, 1986; Gray, 1982; Gunther, 1995; Hui, 1986; Lottes, Weinberg, & Weller, 1993) found consistent results that exposure to pornography produces a variety of substantial negative outcomes. "The results are clear," the review found: "exposure to pornographic material puts one at increased risk for developing sexually deviant tendencies, committing sexual offenses, experiencing difficulties in one's intimate relationships, and accepting the rape myth. In order to promote a healthy and stable society, it is time that we attend to the culmination of sound empirical research."[137]

It's undeniable: pornography is not a harmless, private indulgence but a critical threat to individuals and society. It dangerously alters sexual attitudes and behaviors, heightens aggression, and encourages permissiveness toward child abuse and sexual assault. Those portrayed are often subject to coercion, manipulation, and abuse, and the industry shares inextricable ties to prostitution and human trafficking. As women are treated as sex objects, men are desensitized, and greater sexual permissiveness flourishes, further results are the spread of STDs and a higher number of out-of-wedlock births.

Tying It All Together

Systemic oppression of women, rape, abuse, trafficking, pornography—there seem to be an infinite number of ways that women are and have been preyed upon, mistreated, and exploited for man's gain.

I'm not saying that every man in world history has seen women as less than equal and treated them as such. There are numerous institutions and men throughout history that have worked tirelessly for equal rights for women.

However, we must still draw a sobering conclusion: throughout history, men in power have had a tendency to persecute women, limit their freedoms and powers, and use them for their own devices. This is accomplished through either political or social actions (customs and laws that limit freedoms) or through passive inaction (sitting by and letting women bear society's burdens or blaming them for society's ills). In America today, the number of women suffering abuse at the hands of men is staggering.

How does all of this connect to abortion? There are, certainly, direct links, as exist between pornography, prostitution, and trafficking, or between vulnerable refugees and rape, which all connect to a higher prevalence of unwanted pregnancies and births out of wedlock—many of which are terminated rather than allowed to live.

Yet there are also less obvious connections. In each of these circumstances—whether trafficking or pornography, rape or prostitution—the woman's life is devalued, her rights stripped, so that her worth revolves around her use-value to another person. She becomes a commodity, an object to be used, consumed, and discarded. Rather than enjoying the intrinsic rights of a human being, and rather than being protected as one, she is vulnerable and voiceless, and she becomes a victim as a result.

In the same way, a preborn child lacks the ability to speak for herself, lacks the protection necessary to keep her from harm, and lacks the means to claim her human rights. She is an object—a mass of tissue, to some—a commodity whose worth revolves around her use-value to another person; her very right to live is determined by whether someone else wants her or will find her burdensome. If she is not desired, she is discarded. Although women have been given the choice of whether to abort their children, the context for this decision is determined by a culture of control and oppression that impacts every woman in every nation on the planet.

A picture emerges, then, crossing geographical and temporal boundaries, of men objectifying and taking advantage of women.

Abortion is a manifestation of man's proclivity to exploit women taken to the extreme. Let's now look at how abortion allows men to carry out their grand social plans, as well as exercise their private passions, without commitment or responsibility.

CHAPTER 5

A Woman's Right— Made Legal by Men

W hile our society trumpets abortion as a woman's right and wants to make sure men have no say in it, it is remarkable just how few women were involved in the rise and acceptance of the practice. Considering today's social view that abortion is a right related exclusively to females, men certainly had a lot to do with making sure that right was adopted and passed into law.

In order to understand how men were involved with abortion's 1973 legalization in America, let's first take note that this is not the first time America has faced an abortion crisis.

Abortion in the Nineteenth Century

While many think abortion has only been rampant in America since the 1970s, abortion was common in the 1800s. Detailed statistics are not available, but Edwin Moses Hale, a physician, claimed in 1867 that "two-thirds of the number of conceptions occurring in the United States, and many other civilized countries, are destroyed criminally."[138] Marvin Olasky, author of *Abortion Rites: A Social History of Abortion in America*, estimates that 160,000 abortions were committed annually during the 1860s, a period when 27 million people lived in America.[139]

If the same rate of abortion prevailed today, some 1.86 million abortions would take place each year, given our population of 314 million (instead of the current 1 million–plus abortions annually).

In September 1876, another doctor, Augustus Kinsley Gardner, wrote:

> We look with a shudder upon the poor ignorant Hindoo woman, when from the love for her child which agonizes her mother's heart, in the fervor of her religious enthusiasm sacrifices her beloved offspring at the feet of Juggernaut or in the turbid waves of the sacred Ganges, yet we have not a pang, nor even a word of reprobation, for the human sacrifices of the unborn thousands annually immolated in the city of New York before the blood-worshiped Moloch of fashion.[140]

Though men are primarily responsible for the abortion practice in America today, men were once heavily involved with stemming the abortion tide in the 1800s, as state after state addressed the practice.

Not that abortion had been protected by law. The first abortion-related conviction in America came in 1652 in Maryland, when a Captain William Mitchell was convicted of "adultery, fornication, and murtherous intention" after he forced his twenty-one-year-old bondservant, pregnant with his child, to drink an abortifacient.[141] Such cases were apparently not common. A more common resolution to out-of-wedlock pregnancies was infanticide at birth.

Olasky cites fifty-one infanticide convictions in Massachusetts between 1670 and 1807. But as abortion became more frequent, state legislators responded with statutes to protect the preborn and punish the perpetrators. By 1868, thirty states had criminalized abortion.

Twenty-seven of those state laws, Olasky writes, "punished attempts to induce abortion before quickening."[142]

So while illegal, abortion still became increasingly common in the 1800s. Three groups of people engaged in the social war over abortion, and, over the course of forty or fifty years, achieved some measure of success protecting women and the preborn that would last for a century.

Feminists

Feminists, journalists, and doctors came together in a loose alliance to help America understand the social, medical, and emotional destruction wrought by abortion.

"Most people are unaware that anti-abortion laws enacted in the latter half of the 19th century were a result of advocacy efforts by feminists, who worked in an uneasy alliance with the male-dominated medical profession and the mainstream media," writes Feminists for Life president Serrin Foster. "These women, who had no rights of their own, were equally concerned about the rights of other oppressed groups, such as slaves, children and the unborn."[143]

Unlike many twenty-first-century feminists, the overwhelming majority of early feminists were strongly opposed to abortion and actively worked for its demise.

Noted feminist Elizabeth Cady Stanton understood that abortion devalued women and increased the gender equality gap:

> Abortion is to be classed, as with the killing of newborns, as infanticide . . . There must be a remedy even for such a crying evil as this [abortion]. But where shall it be found, at least where to begin, if not in the complete enfranchisement and elevation of women?[144]

Other notable examples who wrote or spoke out against abortion include Jane Addams, Louisa May Alcott, Pearl S. Buck, and Mary Wollstonecraft.[145] Mary Ann Glendon, the Learned Hand Professor of Law at Harvard University, explains that early feminists fighting for women's rights saw that "the ready availability of abortion would facilitate the sexual exploitation of women." They "regarded free love, abortion and easy divorce as disastrous for women and children."[146]

Perhaps the most well-known early champion of women's rights, Susan B. Anthony, fully understood the negative impact of abortion on women. She argued persuasively that proabortion men were greatly at fault for the harm wrought on women.

> I deplore the horrible crime of child-murder. We want prevention, not merely punishment. We must reach the root of the evil. It [abortion] is practiced by those whose inmost souls revolt from the dreadful deed. All the articles on this subject that I have read have been from men. They denounce women as alone guilty, and never include man in any plans for the remedy. . . . No matter what the motive, love or ease, or a desire to save from suffering the unborn innocent, the woman is awfully guilty who commits the deed, but, oh! thrice guilty is he who drove her to the desperation which impelled her to the crime.[147]

Years later, feminists still understood that abortion demeaned and degraded women. Celebrated feminist Alice Paul, who drafted the Equal Rights Amendment in 1923, opposed abortion. She called abortion "the ultimate exploitation of women."[148] Evelyn Judge, a lifelong friend of

Paul's, said Paul, who died in 1977, once referred to abortion as "killing unborn women."[149]

Contrast that with 1970s feminism, which saw sexual freedom as liberation for both genders. Harvard professor Glendon remarked it "was a puzzling combination of two things that do not ordinarily go together: anger against men and promiscuity; man-hating and man-chasing."[150]

Journalists

Nineteenth-century members of the press were not silent in expressing their views about abortion. John McDowall, an Amherst- and Princeton-educated Christian worker in New York City, founded the Magdalen Society to shelter seduced and abandoned women. In 1833, he established a monthly magazine, *McDowall's Review*, to detail the reality and magnitude of seduction, prostitution, and abortion in Gotham. He revealed that "thousands of children are murdered. Dead infants are frequently found; sometimes in privies, wells, sewers, ponds, docks. . . ."[151] His aggressive reporting of New York's sensual underside angered many. A grand jury rebuked him for creating a "nuisance" that was "degrading to the character of our city."[152]

After McDowall died in 1836, the *National Police Gazette*, led by editor George Wilkes, pledged to provide "full expositions of the infamous practices of abortionists." In an 1846 editorial Wilkes promised that the *Gazette* would "follow up this business until New York is rid of those child destroyers."[153] The campaign continued over the next two decades, but the *Gazette* had more "readership than prestige," according to historian Marvin Olasky, and did not succeed at igniting public furor against the abortion trade.

In 1870, *New York Times* editor Louis Jennings started an antiabortion crusade with an editorial, "The Least of These Little Ones," in which he protested that the "perpetration of infant murder . . . is rank and smells to heaven. Why is there no hint of its punishment?" Jennings commissioned an investigation in which a reporter and "lady friend" visited abortionists, posing as a couple in need of their services. The resulting report told readers that "thousands of human beings" are "murdered before they have seen the light of this world."[154]

Yes; that was in the *New York Times*.

Not all newspapers took an aggressive stance against abortion, but the few that did had a measurable impact on American views and attitudes.

Doctors

In the medical community, certain courageous men rose up, acknowledged the devastation of abortion, and worked tirelessly to promote change in America.

Horatio Robinson Storer, MD, was a leader in the doctor's crusade against abortion. Storer, one of America's first gynecologists, urged the American Medical Association to call for more demanding laws against abortion. As chairman of the AMA Committee on Criminal Abortion, he led preparation of a "Report on Criminal Abortion" that was presented to the Association in 1859.

The report reviewed the scope of abortion in the United States and called for action. It read:

> Our duty is plain. If, by any act, we can effect aught towards the suppression of this crime, it must be done.
> In questions of abstract right, the medical profession

do not acknowledge such words as expediency, time service, cowardice. We are the physical guardians of women; we, alone, thus far, of their offspring in utero. The case is here of life or death—the life or death of thousands—and it depends, almost wholly, upon ourselves.

As a profession we are unanimous in our condemnation of the crime. Mere resolutions to this effect, and nothing more, are therefore useless, evasive, and cruel.

If to want of knowledge on a medical point, the slaughter of countless children now steadily perpetrated in our midst, is to be attributed, it is our duty, as physicians, and as good and true men, both publicly and privately, and by every means in our power, to enlighten this ignorance. [155]

The AMA unanimously accepted the report, which included recommendations for improving laws against abortion. The report and recommendations were sent to the US president, as well as legislatures of each state and territory. It "described the high and increasing rate of criminal abortion, which led to the deaths of 'hundreds of thousands,' and called for the legislators of the state or territory to pass stringent laws to reduce these deaths."[156]

Storer was also active in saving preborn lives through his own literary output. While pursuing legal protection for the preborn, he also actively worked in the lives of families. He published a series of medical journal articles on abortion in *Why Not? A Book for Women*. The book went through four editions and was used by other physicians to counsel women considering abortion. In 1897, Storer cited the role his book had played in helping women to understand the moral and physical implications of abortion. Hundreds of women had changed their minds, he wrote, and were "induced to permit their pregnancy to accomplish its full period."[157]

Storer expressed sympathy for women and pointed out the horror caused by the failure of the medical community to speak out. "The truth is," he wrote, "that our silence has rendered all of us accessory to the crime, and now that the time has come to strip down the veil, and apply the searching caustic or knife to this foul sore in the body politic, the physician needs courage as well as his patient, and may well overflow with regretful sympathy."[158]

Some of Storer's views and approaches limited his effectiveness. However, he was successful at building momentum in the medical community, and numerous other doctors would join him in his stand against abortion. While other doctors stayed silent or were abortionists themselves, the antiabortion group of doctors was able to effect change in American culture and state legislatures.

The efforts of early feminists, doctors, and the media brought success for life-affirming proponents. Frederick Dyer, who wrote the book-length chronicle *The Physicians' Crusade Against Abortion*, recounts, "By 1880, nearly every state and territory had new legislation that made it a serious crime to induce abortions unless the mother's life was in danger. Most of these stringent state laws against abortion were virtually unchanged until *Roe v. Wade* overturned them in 1973."[159]

With laws in place, abortion historian James Mohr wrote, "Between 1880 and 1900 the practice apparently declined in proportion to the total population from what it had been between 1840 and 1880."[160]

Apathy Sets In

Though men and women joined together to protect America from abortion through social and legislative action, apathy eventually set in. The legislative victories attained by 1880 would stand for almost one hundred years, but cracks in the system became evident soon after the laws were passed.

After all, laws were one thing. Prosecution was another. For example, abortionists freely offered their services in the *San Francisco Examiner* during the 1880s and 1890s. The same was true in other cities, including Chicago and St. Louis. Olasky tells about Chicago doctor Rudolph Holmes, who led a 1904 Chicago Medical Society campaign launched to persuade newspapers to "discontinue criminal advertisements or [induce] them to edit the most flagrant violators."[161]

The effort succeeded in ridding Chicago newspapers of abortion solicitations and was imitated in other cities.[162] Still, as Holmes recognized, any victory in the battle was only temporary: "Now that the advertisements are removed the work of the Committee in the future will be to see that they are kept out; in the course of time they undoubtedly will reappear in a new guise. . . ."[163]

Around the turn of the century, the medical profession was wavering in its opposition to abortion. In 1906, the *Journal of the American Medical Association* published Dr. Henry Marcy's assertion that "the product of early impregnation is of so little importance that abortion will not be seriously established as a criminal offense."[164] Dr. William Robinson told a 1911 gathering of the Eastern Medical Society that it was right for unmarried women to abort in certain circumstances. He came out for abortion legalization in the early 1930s, stating that it was "better to permit the removal of a few inanimate cells" than to have "unwanted" children born.[165]

In 1936, Missouri gynecologist Dr. Frederick Taussig wrote *Abortion, Spontaneous and Induced*, a 536-page treatment of the abortion issue praised by *Time* magazine as an "authoritative" and "milestone text."[166] Historian Marvin Olasky called it the "most influential pro-abortion book of the 1930s" and noted that Taussig endorsed legal abortion for instances when "the mother is physically depleted by childbearing and poverty" or "clearly irresponsible."[167] Taussig claimed that 8,000 to 10,000 women died annually from abortion and formulated an argument for abortion that would be used in decades to come, contending "that more consideration must be given to the right of women to control their own bodies."[168]

Taussig's numbers were faulty. Six years later, he confessed that his 1936 book, which also claimed that 681,000 abortions occurred annually, had used "the wildest estimates as to the number of abortions and the number of abortion deaths."[169] He gave a new estimate at a 1942 medical conference of no more than 5,000 abortion deaths annually, but that claim was not tied to any hard statistical evidence either. In any case, the danger to women from abortion dropped sharply after the introduction of penicillin in the mid-1940s. So much so that, whatever the true number of abortion-related maternal deaths in 1942, by 1957 Planned Parenthood reported just 260 deaths linked to abortion in America.[170]

The same 1942 National Committee on Maternal Health-sponsored conference where Taussig cut his abortion death estimate by half heard support for abortion, with one speaker suggesting, "the ultimate decision should be hers."[171] At a 1955 Planned Parenthood conference on abortion, Yale psychiatry professor Theodore Lidz declared, "[A]bortion is preferable to the birth of a child that might be injurious to the well-being of the mother. . . ."[172] Participants at the Planned Parenthood gathering concluded that the "mounting approval of psychiatric, humanitarian, and eugenic indications for the legal termination of pregnancy" justified a more relaxed legal environment.[173]

While medical professionals refashioned their attitudes toward abortion, the press shifted its approach, as well. Nineteenth-century coverage by the *New York Times* and the *National Police Gazette* had given readers sensational and lurid accounts of predatory abortionists who enriched themselves at the cost of the lives of young women. That changed in the 1930s and 1940s as newspaper accounts distinguished between mercenary and corrupt abortionists and the more humanitarian sort who committed abortion out of compassion. The press, Olasky writes, began to present abortion as an issue in which the "problem was not abortion but the 'unscrupulous abortionist.'"[174]

One of the most evocative and influential events, which generated national press coverage and presented abortion in a sympathetic light, was the case of Mrs. Sherri Finkbine, a pregnant Arizona mother of four. Fearful that the thalidomide in her sleeping pills would create shortened limbs or other defects in her preborn child, Finkbine unsuccessfully sought an abortion in Arizona and ultimately traveled to Sweden for the procedure. The press played up her "plight," and an *Atlanta Constitution* editorial recommended that the "nation ought to have a look at their abortion laws in light of what they did to her."[175] A late 1962 Gallup Poll found that 52 percent of respondents thought Finkbine had "done the right thing" in aborting her child, while 32 percent disagreed with her and 16 percent had no opinion.[176]

Three years later, the *New York Times* came out for liberalized abortion laws, editorializing that limiting abortion to instances aimed at saving the life of the mother "is certainly an example of man's inhumanity to man—or, more directly, to woman."[177]

Turning Back to Abortion

In the late 1960s, these shifts in attitude led to the relaxation of state abortion laws. Unlike their predecessors, contemporary feminists were recruited by men to support abortion.

Abortion laws softened in 1967 as Colorado, California, and North Carolina all passed legislation legalizing abortion for pregnancies that resulted from rape or incest, for life-threatening situations, and for pregnancies of severely handicapped children. Another nine states would enact similar legislation by 1970: Arkansas, Delaware, Georgia, Kansas, Maryland, New Mexico, Oregon, South Carolina, and Virginia.[178]

The first state to offer unrestricted abortions was New York in 1970. Abortion became legal there during the first twenty-four weeks of pregnancy. Hawaii, Alaska, and Washington soon followed. One year later, in 1971, the famed *Roe v. Wade* case first came to trial. When the verdict was handed down in 1973, all state laws regulating abortion were stricken, and abortion on demand became the uniform standard across all fifty states.

Race toward Legalization

How did abortion's legalization come so swiftly? How did we move from the near-universal prohibition of abortion to abortion on demand across the entire nation?

Dr. Bernard Nathanson, a prominent figure in the abortion rights movement, provides tremendous insight into the strategy behind the success.

He met journalist Lawrence Lader, later called the father of the abortion-rights movement by feminist Betty Friedan,[179] at a dinner party in 1967, where they discovered their mutual passion for abortion. "We began to talk, and the conversation lasted eight years," Nathanson recalled. "[I]n that span of time, every abortion law in the United States was struck down, the lines between pro- and antiabortionists were drawn, and the battle joined."[180]

He and Lader cofounded NARAL (originally the National Association for the Repeal of Abortion Laws and now known as NARAL Pro-Choice America), which became the primary organization in the fight to legalize abortion. Nathanson remembers Lader met him "at the right moment":

> I was upset over the health hazard from illegal abortion, and had moved from disillusionment to cynicism to anger at the inequity and hypocrisy in the abortion business. . . . Lader never misrepresented his radical purpose: total abolition of abortion restrictions. . . . It did not seem a time for careful analysis of the issues.[181]

Lawrence Lader's crusade to legalize abortion was heavily inspired by Margaret Sanger, the leading figure in the birth control movement. He wrote an authorized biography of Sanger in 1955 and said the Planned Parenthood founder "undoubtedly was the greatest influence on my life." Sanger's belief in "inviolable personhood" led him to believe that the mother has the sole right over what happens inside her body and that she "controlled the fetus she was nurturing."[182]

Betty Friedan, mother of the modern feminist movement, once asked Lader why he took up the cause of abortion legalization. It was because of Sanger, Lader explained, quoting from Sanger's 1920 work, *Woman and the New Race*: "No woman can call herself free who does not own and control her own body. No woman can call herself free until she can choose consciously whether she will or will not be a mother."[183]

For Lader, the right to abortion was a moral cause on par with the abolition of slavery in the 1800s. "Both involved fundamental moral and religious positions that collided with the entrenched interests of their time," he wrote. And both, he added, "had been created by laws which were blatantly in conflict with basic rights seemingly protected by the Constitution. . . ."[184]

Lader, who gave much of his life to rewriting America's abortion law and expanding access to abortion, argued that laws against abortion "denied women control over their own bodies and procreation by forcing them to bear children against their will."[185] He gave little attention, if any, to the moral status of the preborn and his or her right to be born.

Lader's influential 1966 book, *Abortion*, was a sweeping survey of "the laws and practices governing abortion in the U.S. and around the world." Justice Harry Blackmun cited Lader's book eight times in his 1973 Supreme Court ruling overturning all abortion laws in the United States and awarding women the right to choose to end the lives of their preborn children.

The leading figures behind the abortion legalization movement were predominantly male. Abortion historian David Garrow writes that Pat Maginnis, a California woman actively working to repeal abortion laws in the 1960s, "rued the low level of activity on behalf of liberalization, particularly by women, and told [American Civil Liberties Union cofounder] Morris Ernst that 'the men have given us the greatest support.'"[186]

Lader realized he needed women's voices. Nathanson sheds light on how Lader recruited women into the effort to legalize abortion. He recounts how Lader remarked, "If we're going to move abortion out of the books and into the streets, we're going to have to recruit the feminists."[187]

Nathanson initially thought that was a mistake: "I figured that if the feminists appeared to take over, the necessary abortion reform would be dismissed by moderates without a fair hearing. I was dead wrong, of course. Lader's marriage with the feminists was a brilliant tactic."[188]

Nathanson and Lader had a specific agenda, the legalization of abortion, but realized they needed to use the appropriate women to gain acceptance in the various states. The question became, then, would the face of the organization be male or female?

"For president, we needed someone pledged to activism and politically astute," Nathanson wrote. "Of course it had to be a woman, though Larry figured to actually run N.A.R.A.L. as chairman of the Executive Committee."[189]

In other words, men would continue to run the organization, while a woman was to be the public face of it. Nathanson recalled their political calculations:

> "We've got to keep the women out in front," [Larry] asserted. "You know what I mean."
>
> Yes, I did. And that made eminent political sense, too.
>
> "And some blacks. Black women especially. Why are they so damn slow to see the importance of this whole movement to themselves?"[190]

Even the honorary officers "had to be women, not only to solidify our ties to the feminists, but to rally politically uncommitted women," Nathanson writes. He and Lader "must have sifted through fifty or more names for honorary president" seeking a "white Establishment figure ... and also a black ... and also a female."[191] Ultimately, Shirley Chisholm, the first black woman elected to Congress, and Dr. Lester Brimlow, president of the American Public Health Association, were tabbed to share the honorary presidency.

Lader and Nathanson recruited Betty Friedan, the cofounder in 1966 of the National Organization of Women, to "join us in the [abortion] revolution,"[192] and she joined the founding board of NARAL.

Recall that nineteenth-century feminists were staunchly against abortion; they realized abortion harmed and exploited women. The twentieth-century feminist movement did not, at first, support abortion either. Rosemary Oelrich Bottcher, a past president of Feminists for Life, writes:

> The first edition of Betty Friedan's seminal book, *The Feminine Mystique*, did not even mention abortion. Legalizing abortion was not on the newborn NOW's list of issues. In his 1979 book, *Aborting America*, Dr. Nathanson recalled Lader saying, "... Friedan has got to put her troops into this thing—while she still has control of them."
>
> When I met Nathanson at the National Right to Life convention in June of 1986, he told me that they convinced the leaders of NOW that easy access to legal abortion was essential to ameliorating the problems that were thwarting the well-being of women, the problems that Friedan had identified in her book.
>
> "We got them to see legal abortion as a civil rights issue, a basic women's rights issue," Nathanson explained.[193]

Thus men conspired to successfully convince leading feminists to include abortion on their agenda as a fix to their other feminist concerns.

Though Friedan would live out the rest of her days as a supporter of abortion, she became critical of NARAL's and NOW's politicized focus on it. "To my mind," she wrote in 2000, "there is far too much focus on abortion. . . . [I]n recent years I've gotten a little uneasy about the movement's narrow focus on abortion as if it were the single, all-important issue for women, when it's not."[194]

In 1981, Friedan even suggested that feminists "join forces with all who have true reverence for life, including Catholics who oppose abortion, and fight for the choice to have children."[195]

Other writers and historians recognize that the abortion agenda was driven by men who, in turn, convinced and used women to gain support and credibility. "Elitist men have always been the demographic most strongly in support of unrestricted abortion, though they needed vocal women to do their bidding," observes writer Stella Morabito.[196]

In 1971, demographer Judith Blake looked at abortion and public opinion from 1960 to 1970 and reached the surprising conclusion that abortion legalization was not most supported by the "less advantaged and by women." Instead, "Legalized abortion is supported most strongly by the non-Catholic, male, well-educated 'establishment.'"[197] Blake also said, with some understatement, "Upper-class men have much to gain and very little to lose by an easing of legal restrictions against abortion."[198]

And so America, which had fought to protect women and children from abortion in the 1800s, capitulated on that effort in the 1900s. And the effort to legalize abortion was primarily and aggressively driven by men.

The question is, why? Dr. Nathanson had his reason, and it was somewhat idealistic—he was concerned about the health and well-being of women getting "back-alley" abortions. He saw the legalization of abortion as a means to protect women's health.

Still, Nathanson, the cofounder of NARAL, eventually had a change of heart and spent his later years denouncing abortion. He worked to restore America to a culture that respected both women and the pre-born. In an interview held in 1986, Nathanson shared:

"I ran the largest abortion clinic in the world for two years. I had no conflicts whatsoever at the time I was doing the abortions. I changed my mind because the new scientific data which we were getting from advanced technology persuaded me that we could not indiscriminately continue to slaughter what was demonstrably a human being."[199]

Even while supporting abortion, Nathanson described a desire to protect women and their health. Yet were all men as altruistic? Were men fighting so hard for abortion because they were concerned about women's health?

Was it for women's rights? Were these courageous men who saw abortion as a means to elevate women, bringing them to true equality with men?

Or was it something else? Were there other agendas behind man's insistence on creating an abortion culture in America?

PART 2
Men Oppress with It

CHAPTER 6
Weeding the Garden

While a few men were truly concerned about women's health and saw the legalization of abortion as a means to protect women, the overwhelming majority of male abortion advocates had other motivations: social change and personal sexual behaviors.

On the societal level, the two primary drivers of abortion are population control and eugenics, which often go hand in hand. On the personal level, the driver is male sexual freedom from responsibility or consequence. Women are either being used to advance social agendas or they are being used as sex objects. In either case, women are being exploited as tools to further promote mostly male agendas.

Population control is the process of maintaining or slowing population growth by decree or practice. Let's look for a moment at an example: China's One Child Policy, which changed January 1, 2016, to a Two Child Policy.

Many in the mainstream media praised the change, with some even acknowledging the necessity of the original policy; according to the *Los Angeles Times*, "Without [the One Child Policy], China might have faced catastrophe,"[200] while the *Boston Globe* quoted a professor who argued that the original policy was "a good thing."[201] Even among its critics, a number have lauded China's revocation of the One Child Policy as a step forward for human rights.

It is nothing of the sort. Under the system, China employs an arduous process of parents obtaining birth permits, a system of paid informants, and ultrasound checks to ensure a woman's IUD is still in place.[202] Friends, coworkers, and neighbors are encouraged to report on each other if a violation is suspected. If a violation is discovered, the parents must pay steep fines that many are unable to afford; if they are unable to pay the fines, the women may legally be dragged from their houses, strapped down, and their babies forcibly aborted. The women may also be sterilized against their will. They have no recourse to the legal system; the courts will not hear such cases. All of this continues under the Two Child Policy.

As blind activist Chen Guangchen tweeted:

"This is nothing to be happy about. First the #CCP would kill any baby after one. Now they will kill any baby after two."[203]

China's efforts at population control have had other horrific consequences in addition to these violations of human rights, such as what's been called the "gendercide" of millions of females. Due to sex-selective abortion and infanticide, the ratio of women to men has left 37 million Chinese men without women to marry, resulting in a spike in sex trafficking and sex slavery in China and its neighboring countries.[204] China has seen almost 200 million sterilizations, an epidemic of child kidnapping, and the widespread abandonment of girl babies.[205] This will continue under the new policy, as many parents will still abort any preborn girls in preference of boys. Another result is that China's working-age population has plummeted and their birth rate has dropped far below sustainable levels. Their economy is suffering the consequences, which is the real reason behind the update to a Two Child Policy.

Although many male babies have also been aborted as part of these policies, overwhelmingly these measures impact females—the mothers who face abortion and sterilization against their will, the millions of preborn girls aborted or killed after birth, and the girls and women sold into sexual slavery. This illustrates an important point: that efforts at population control *always* target specific populations. This is why these efforts go hand-in-hand with another, similar agenda—eugenics.

Eugenics is the applied science of weeding out less desirable populations in favor of more desirable populations. In Western history, it generally refers to intentionally decreasing or eliminating a particular race. In recent history, the Nazi holocaust is a well-known, egregious example of applied eugenics.

Eugenics is basically an extension or subset of population control. The rise of abortion in America can be tied directly to both of these social agendas.

"Civil libertarians and feminists were certainly in the picture when it came to the legalization of abortion, but in many cases they were handy instruments of the eugenicists and population controllers," writes Mary Meehan, a senior editor of *Human Life Review*. Abortion advocates had deep-pocketed friends, receiving "enormous aid from the American establishment or 'power elite.'"[206]

Understanding man's role in the legalization of abortion in America requires a closer look at the eugenics movement. Although they may seem separate topics on the surface, population control, eugenics, and abortion are intimately connected, as all three concern the intentional reduction of a specific people group. This is the reason that the same ideas, individuals, and organizations emerge repeatedly across all three movements. For this closer look, we turn our attention to the $1 billion nonprofit phenomenon known as Planned Parenthood.

Margaret Sanger

In 1916, a soft-spoken, passionate female activist opened up the very first birth control center in New York City. Not only did she and a group of friends coin the term "birth control," she went on to start an organization known as the American Birth Control League in 1922. That organization eventually became Planned Parenthood, the most powerful name in birth control and abortion.

Her name was Margaret Sanger, and she was one of the very few prominent female leaders in the movement toward legal abortion, so her background is worth reviewing. In fact, men with both social and personal abortion agendas heavily influenced her views, approach, and tactics.

Sanger started her career as a nurse, working with extremely poor populations. She viewed unplanned children as a core cause of poverty, misery, disease, and death. Poor women pleaded with her to help them limit their families, whether it was for their own physical health, the economic survival of their families, or their own mental well-being. After giving up nursing, she committed her life to educating women about birth control so they were empowered to dictate the size of their families. She saw birth control as a necessary and vital remedy to numerous social ills.

Sanger, the publisher of *The Birth Control Review* and, before that, *The Woman Rebel*, was also a tireless champion of eugenics. She wanted to rid society of "human weeds" and wrote, in 1925, "We must clear the way for a better world; we must cultivate our garden."[207]

Birth control was her original method of choice, but her views broadened over the years. She endorsed the segregation of "every feeble-minded girl or woman . . . especially of the moron class" during their fertile years and concluded in her 1922 book, *The Pivot of Civilization*, that sterilization was an even better option. Since "segregation carried out for one or two generations would give us only partial control of the problem," she wrote, ". . . we prefer the policy of immediate sterilization, of making sure that parenthood is absolutely prohibited to the feeble-minded."[208]

"The most urgent problem," according to Sanger, "is how to limit and discourage the over-fertility of the mentally and physically defective." And coercion, she made clear, was a tool to be considered: "Possibly drastic and Spartan methods may be forced upon American society if it continues complacently to encourage the chance and chaotic breeding that has resulted from our stupid, cruel sentimentalism."[209]

Sanger was not alone in her extreme eugenic views, nor did she arrive at her conclusions on her own. The founding board of the Birth Control League included at least two male eugenicists, Lothrop Stoddard and C. C. Little. Stoddard was the author of *The Rising Tide of Color Against White World-Supremacy*, a startling book that divided humanity by color—whites, yellows, blacks, browns, and reds. In it, he warned of a "dreaded" tide of color, which would "swamp whole populations and turn countries now white into colored man's lands irretrievably lost to the white world."[210] Little was a president of the American Eugenics Society.

Another Birth Control League board member was American Eugenics Society cofounder Harry Laughlin. He also served as director of the Eugenics Records Office, America's first major eugenics research institution, from its inception in 1910 to 1939, when it closed its doors. Laughlin drafted a "model law" for compulsory sterilization, which the Reichstag of Nazi Germany used as the basis for its Law for the Prevention of Hereditarily Diseased Offspring, passed in 1933. Laughlin was awarded an honorary degree in 1936 by the University of Heidelberg for his work on behalf of the "science of racial cleansing."[211]

Over in Britain, eugenicists George Bernard Shaw and H. G. Wells were influential friends of Sanger.

Shaw, in 1910, acknowledged that "[a] part of eugenics politics would finally land us in an extensive use of the lethal chamber. A great many people would have to be put out of existence simply because it wastes other people's time to look after them," and in 1934 he wrote, "The moment we face it frankly we are driven to the conclusion that the community has a right to put a price on the right to live in it. . . . If they are not fit to live, kill them in a decent human way. Is it any wonder that some of us are driven to prescribe the lethal chamber as the solution. . .?"[212]

H. G. Wells, who composed the foreword to Sanger's book *The Pivot of Civilization*, wrote in 1902, "In the new vision death is no inexplicable horror, no pointless terminal terror to the miseries of life. . . . The men of the New Republic will not be squeamish, either, in facing or inflicting death, because they will have a fuller sense of the possibilities of life than we possess. They will have an ideal that will make killing worth while. . . . This thing, this euthanasia of the weak and sensual, is possible. On the principles that will probably animate the predominant classes of the new time, it will be permissible, and I have little or no doubt that in the future it will be planned and achieved."[213]

Of this, Wells was quite right—it would be both planned and achieved in the 1930s and '40s.

It is no wonder that Sanger would describe what she saw as the result of an uncultivated garden: "We are paying for and even submitting to the dictates of an ever increasing, unceasingly spawning class of human beings who never should have been born at all."[214]

Havelock Ellis

However, the most profound male influence on Sanger was British sexologist Havelock Ellis. A prolific author on human sexuality, Ellis wrote the six-volume *Studies in the Psychology of Sex* and authored the first British medical textbook on homosexuality. He married at thirty-two years of age, though it was an unconventional relationship. His wife was a lesbian,[215] and they spent much of their time in separate residences.[216] He was also a eugenicist who served as president of the Galton Institute and vice president of the Eugenics Education Society.

In order to understand Havelock Ellis, it's important to note his connection to Francis Galton, of whom Ellis was a "beloved disciple."[217] Galton's name is familiar to evolutionists, as Galton was the cousin of Charles Darwin, the author of *On the Origin of Species by Means of Natural Selection, or the Preservation of Favoured Races in the Struggle for Life* (later shortened to *On the Origin of Species*). Galton was deeply impacted by Darwin's work, and Darwin's evolutionary theory wove its way into Galton's mind-set and writings. The original title of Darwin's work displays the natural tie of evolutionary theory to eugenics, as the latter is based on the preservation of some races and the diminishment of others.

Ellis, heavily influenced by Galton, adopted a very similar philosophy. Darwin's survival-of-the-fittest approach is a necessary key in eugenics, but instead of operating by blind chance, the genetically well-endowed manage the human stock for optimal outcomes. Ellis discussed one way to do so in "The Sterilization of the Unfit," an article that appeared in 1909 in the first issue of the *British Eugenics Review*.[218] In 1912, Ellis advocated comprehensive record-keeping of "all personal facts, biological and mental, normal and morbid . . . if we are to have a real guide as to those persons who are most fit, or most unfit to carry on the race."[219]

He advocated the practice of voluntary sterilization of the weak-minded, claiming that "the feeble minded, realising their own weakness, are willing and even anxious to be in this way protected against themselves."[220]

Havelock Ellis and Margaret Sanger would form an intimate friendship that lasted for years, during which he was both her "mentor and lover," according to Sanger biographer Madeline Gray.[221] After Ellis died in 1939, Sanger did a radio interview and extolled his character and contributions. She recalled with reverent awe first meeting him at his home in England in 1914. When Ellis opened the door, "He seemed like a god, with his tall, slender figure, and his great shock of white hair, his massive head, his wide expressive mouth and deep-set eyes. . . ."[222]

Sanger was taken by Ellis's staunch devotion to women's rights and their liberation, saying in the interview that he "helped to usher in a new day of womankind. . . . He threw the weight of his vast knowledge and influence into advancing the cause of women's freedom, and to women everywhere he seemed a heaven-sent liberator."[223]

By Sanger's own admission, Ellis had a profound impact on her education, studies, and approach to eugenics. The British eugenicist, she said, "guided my early studies and directed my reading for a year and a half in that famous historical spot, the British Museum," where she met regularly with him.[224]

Was She or Wasn't She?

During their time together, Sanger leaned heavily on Ellis to help her craft her strategy related to birth control and eugenics. He persuaded her, as a tactical move, to drop her support for abortion, telling her that industrial society was not ready to cross that threshold.[225]

Before taking Ellis's advice, Sanger had already announced the "right to destroy" and published a pamphlet treating abortion as a form of birth control. Sanger announced in 1914 what she called the "Rebel Woman Claim," which included the "right to be an unmarried mother," the "right to create," and the "right to destroy."[226]

She was more explicit in a sixteen-page pamphlet first published in 1914 called "Family Limitation." For women who suspected that conception had occurred, Sanger recommended drinking quinine—a dangerous prescription, which can lead to renal failure—to "prevent the ovum from making its nest in the lining of the womb." But if that fails, "then the only remedy is an abortion."

Sanger went on to endorse abortion as a method of birth control in the same publication, telling readers:

> When once one has been convinced that an abortion is necessary, do not indulge in medicines of any kind. They only weaken the system, and require a much greater length of time to recuperate. Never allow a pregnancy to run over a month. If you are going to have an abortion, make up your mind to it in the first stages, and have it done. On the other hand, there is often a feeling of the strongest desire to continue with the pregnancy. It is for each woman to decide this for herself, but act at once, whichever way you decide.[227]

Advised by Ellis to pursue a more politically expedient course, Sanger later promoted contraception as an allegedly safe alternative to abortion and denounced abortion publicly.[228]

The contradiction between Sanger's initial support of abortion and her autobiography are telling. Originally published in 1938, Sanger noted the dangers and truth about abortion several times and advised against it:

> I still had that naïve trust that when the facts were known, the Government would not willfully condemn millions of women to death, misery, or abortion which left them physically damaged and spiritually crippled.[229]

> All the while their discussions had been proceeding, the people themselves had been and still were blindly, desperately, practicing birth control by the most barbaric methods—infanticide, abortion, and other crude ways.[230]

> To each group we explained simply what contraception was; that abortion was the wrong way—no matter how early it was performed it was the taking of a life. . . .[231]

Margaret Sanger was apparently convinced by Havelock Ellis and was not an active abortion promoter or advocate in her later years. Despite being the founder of the organization that would become Planned Parenthood, she labeled abortion "spiritually crippl[ing]," "barbaric," "the wrong way," and "the taking of a life."

It wasn't women who would aggressively push for the legalization of abortion in America. It was men.

In 1943, the Birth Control Federation of America, a successor organization to Sanger's original American Birth Control League, became the Planned Parenthood Federation of America. But the name change didn't alter its eugenicist agenda. A 1943 Planned Parenthood list of goals stated the group's intent to "foster selective pregnancy . . . and . . . seek to offer the eugenically unsound means to avoid bringing offspring into the world who would become social liabilities."[232]

In 1945, another similar outline of Planned Parenthood goals read, in part, "The weak and defective compose an alarming proportion of our present population. . . ." The solution was "providing reliable contraceptive advice for those who, because of disease, defectiveness or deficiency, are unfitted to bear children."[233]

But as Nazi horrors became known in America, public opinion swung against eugenics, requiring its advocates to play their cards much closer to their vests. C. P. Blacker, chosen by Sanger to be the founding president of the International Planned Parenthood Federation, endorsed what he called "crypto-eugenics." He understood that eugenics would only be advanced if the actual agenda was hidden, saying, "You seek to fulfill the aims of eugenics without disclosing what you are really aiming at and without mentioning the word."[234]

Havelock Ellis was very much the master planner behind Sanger's passions, as she herself proudly admitted. And though the "right to destroy," which she endorsed in 1914, was not realized in her lifetime, her successor at Planned Parenthood saw that right arrive with the Supreme Court's 1973 *Roe v. Wade* ruling.

Alan Guttmacher

Just three years after Sanger's death in 1966, Planned Parenthood adopted abortion legalization as a corporate policy. Its president, Dr. Alan Guttmacher, an obstetrician-gynecologist, was, as early as the 1940s, one of the nation's first physicians to move toward legalized abortion.

Guttmacher called for liberalizing abortion laws at the American Birth Control Federation's 1942 annual meeting, saying, "[T]he patent hypocrisy and holier-than-thou attitude of the medical profession in regard to this problem is revolting."[235]

In 1962, Guttmacher left his post as chief of obstetrics and gynecology at Mt. Sinai Hospital to become Planned Parenthood president. Guttmacher was out in front of his organization on abortion, writing in 1974 that he "took this [abortion legalization] position long before it became Planned Parenthood policy in 1969."[236]

As with almost every man associated with the promotion and legalization of abortion, Guttmacher was a population-control and eugenics advocate, serving as a vice president of the American Eugenic Society. Like many others, he was willing to use force to achieve population control. "Each country," he said in 1969, "will have to decide its own form of coercion, and determine when and how it should be employed. At present, the means are compulsory sterilization and compulsory abortion. Perhaps someday a way of enforcing compulsory birth control will be feasible."[237]

Guttmacher observed that it's best to use camouflage when seeking to achieve population control on the international stage: "If you're going to curb population, it's extremely important not to have it done by the damned Yankees, but by the UN. Because the thing is, then it's not considered genocide." As Guttmacher told an interviewer, "If the United States goes to the black man or the yellow man and says slow down your reproductive rate, we're immediately suspected of having ulterior motives to keep the white man dominant in the world. If you send in a colorful UN force, you've got much better leverage."[238]

As Ellis, Sanger, and eventually Guttmacher continued their rise to prominence in the twentieth century, other men of tremendous wealth and power were advancing their abortion agendas.

The Money Men

Billionaire John D. Rockefeller III and military leader/philanthropist Frederick Osborn launched the Population Council in 1952, a foundation that worked diligently to convince government leaders in poor nations that they had population problems. They then provided potential solutions to those governments.

The solutions included distributing intrauterine devices (IUDs) and other contraceptive/abortifacient (abortion causing) devices in so-called third-world nations. Though population control was their public concern, their private agenda was eugenics.

Osborn tipped off a correspondent that the Population Council was pursuing a crypto-eugenics agenda by spending large sums on IUDs, adding, "We have felt this could be done far more effectively in the name of Population Control than in the name of eugenics. . . . Personally, I think it is the most important practical eugenic measure ever taken."[239]

John D. Rockefeller III was a self-proclaimed eugenicist, and it ran in the family. Both his father, John D. Rockefeller Jr., and his grandfather, oil magnate John D. Rockefeller, were members of the American Eugenics Society. John D. Rockefeller III contributed heavily during the Depression years to keep it solvent.

Abortion was also on the Rockefeller agenda. In 1967, John D. Rockefeller III told his sister, "[T]he matter of abortion is the principal remaining area in the population field which has not been given the attention that it should."[240]

In 1970, it was New York governor Nelson Rockefeller, John D. Rockefeller III's brother, who signed into law a measure allowing abortion for any reason up to six months gestation. Two years later, Governor Rockefeller vetoed a measure to repeal that law.

John D. Rockefeller III also supported the Association for the Study of Abortion, which pressed for the legalization of abortion and included other major eugenicists such as Guttmacher, Harvard Divinity School professor and situation ethics advocate Joseph Fletcher, and abortion statistician Christopher Tietze.

Frederick Osborn was the key strategist of the American Eugenics Society and the first president of the Population Council. Well before surgical abortions became a major issue, Osborn advocated research on chemical abortions and the Population Council's distribution of abortifacient IUDs. His agenda and motivations are clear, as he said in 1974, "Birth control and abortion are turning out to be the great eugenic advances of our time. If they had been advanced for eugenic reasons it would have retarded or stopped their acceptance."[241]

The population-control / eugenics movement tied logically and inevitably into abortion. For example, Stanford biology professor and population alarmist Paul Ehrlich issued a warning of coming doom in his 1968 bestseller, *The Population Bomb*. Ehrlich predicted that "hundreds of millions of people are going to starve to death" in the 1970s because of famines tied to overpopulation and listed abortion as one way to defuse the bomb. He argued for the legalization of abortion in the United States and wrote that "in many cases abortion is much more desirable than childbirth."[242]

President Richard Nixon appointed a population commission in 1970, which studied the issue for two years and recommended, among other things, public funding for abortion "on request." The chairman of the committee was none other than John D. Rockefeller III, with numerous other Population Council members and eugenicists on the commission or related staff.

The commission, as writer Mary Meehan notes, asked

for more research on fertility control and more subsidy of contraception and sterilization; [it] support[ed] sex education and 'population education' in the schools; and recommend[ed] a national average of two children per couple.[243]

Eugenics Applied to Minorities

Historically, eugenics targeted poor populations and minorities. Though the modern media downplays the role of racism and gender discrimination in eugenics, the words of the movement's founders are quite clear. Francis Galton, for example, wrote in 1904 that "while most barbarous races disappear, some, like the negro, do not,"[244] and Sanger associate Lothrop Stoddard issued a dire warning in 1922 about the "rising tide of color against white-world supremacy." Eugenicist Madison Grant's popular book, *The Passing of the Great Race*, inveighed against the "social and racial crime" of interracial marriage and said, "[T]he law against miscegenation [interracial marriage] must be greatly extended if the higher races are to be maintained."[245]

In his landmark 1944 examination of American race relations, Swedish eugenicist Gunnar Myrdal claimed, without a shred of evidence, that "all white Americans agree that, if the Negro is to be eliminated, he must be eliminated slowly so as not to hurt any individual living Negroes."[246]

But how could that slow fade of African Americans from the population be achieved? After dismissing outright elimination, deportation, voluntary emigration, and keeping the black death rate high, Myrdal concludes, "The only possible way of decreasing Negro population is by means of controlling fertility."[247] One option offered by Myrdal in *The American Dilemma* is to provide the African American population with birth control—lots of it. Myrdal suggests "birth control facilities could be extended relatively more to Negroes than whites."[248]

Margaret Sanger's "Negro Project" was an effort to expand the distribution of contraceptives to African Americans. Her real agenda may have been similar to Myrdal's claim about the common ambition of all whites. In private correspondence with fellow eugenicist Dr. Clarence Gamble, Sanger wrote, "We do not want the word to go out that we want to exterminate the Negro population and the minister is the man who can straighten that idea out if it ever occurs to any of their more rebellious members."[249]

For his part, Gamble proposed recruiting black doctors to serve with ministers as advocates for the birth control campaign. "There is great danger that [the project] will fail because the Negroes think it a plan for extermination," Gamble wrote Sanger. "Hence let's appear to let the colored run it. . . ."[250]

Whatever the motive behind Sanger's birth control initiative to black Americans, it's disturbing to realize that African Americans, who now make up 12.8 percent of the population, have 35.4 percent of all abortions. Even more striking is the fact that the abortion rate—the number of abortions per 1,000 women—is almost four times greater among black women (32.5) than white women (8.5).[251]

One reason for the dramatic difference in abortion rates may be the higher concentration of Planned Parenthood abortion facilities near black neighborhoods, possibly following Myrdal's suggestion. An analysis done by Life Issues Institute researcher Susan Enouen compared the location of Planned Parenthood abortion facilities with Census Bureau data and found that "62% of Planned Parenthood abortion facilities are within walking distance (2 miles) of relatively high African American populations."[252]

Another similar analysis conducted by Life Dynamics checked the zip codes of minority neighborhoods against the locations of abortion facilities and found that 83 percent of facilities that perform or refer for abortions are in minority neighborhoods. As Life Dynamics president Mark Crutcher put it, "The numbers make it clear that the African-American and Hispanic communities have been targeted, and logic makes it clear that this did not happen coincidentally or unintentionally."[253]

Population Control and Women

Despite the fact that global population growth is slowing and may begin to decline within our lifetime,[254] funding for population-control measures seems to be a well that never runs dry. Notable names such as Rockefeller, Ford, Mellon, and Packard are among the many foundations that have historically supported this movement. New money for population control is coming from, among others, Warren Buffet, Bill Gates, Ted Turner, and George Soros.[255] These men and others, including Michael Bloomberg, David Rockefeller, and Oprah Winfrey, gathered in May 2009 for a "billionaires' club" summit to discuss their favorite causes and settled on world population as their primary concern.

One individual at the meeting told the *London Times*, "This is something so nightmarish that everyone in this group agreed it needs big-brain answers. They need to be independent of government agencies, which are unable to head off the disaster we all see looming."[256]

Population control is often packaged in the rhetoric of "sexual and reproductive rights," or as preventing unplanned pregnancies, but there is an undeniable power dynamic at play any time populations are managed.

It's easy to get angry at the thought of billionaires flying their Lear jets to a meeting where they determine which people groups should be curtailed—because, at the core, that is what population control decides. But a degree of eugenicist philosophy is occurring every time any organization seeks to control populations.

According to Merriam-Webster, a "population" is "a group of people or animals of a particular kind that live in a place." Meanwhile, their dictionary defines "eugenics" as "a science that tries to improve the human race by controlling which people become parents."[257] By definition, then, any measure of population control is a form of eugenics in action—an effort to improve humanity by controlling the offspring of certain people. The only way it could be anything else were if its measures were employed equally, across the board, to all people groups; since a population is by definition a people group of a particular kind, and because these measures (such as abortion or sterilization) are always employed against particular people groups, the conclusion is clear:

Population control and eugenics are two sides of the same coin . . . no matter how many coins you might have.

Population control is also commonly linked to environmental actions and climate change. As Hillary Clinton commented in 2009, "[I]t's rather odd to talk about climate change and what we must do to stop and prevent the ill effects without talking about population and family planning." That year, the Senate Appropriations Committee approved a bill that allotted $628 million to "family planning/reproductive health" as it links to climate change.[258]

Organizations that globally advocate for abortions as a part of "family planning" and population management—such as Pathfinder International, which the Clinton Global Initiative supports—frequently list environmental interactions as an area of concern.

China's family planning policies continue to be justified in terms of environmental impact, much as they were in 2009 at the UN climate conference in Copenhagen, when Zhao Baige, a senior member of the Chinese delegation, asserted that the One Child Policy had saved the world from millions of tons of annual CO2 emissions.[259] On October 29, 2015, the *Los Angeles Times* quoted a "reproduction and childbirth ethics expert" from the University of East Anglia who stated, "It is sensible for countries to have explicit policies on reproduction just as they do on carbon emissions and other phenomena that affect the population on a large scale. China's one-child policy was a logical choice at the time, though perhaps crudely enforced."[260] That horrific human-rights abuses continue to be justified by their impact on the environment is hugely troublesome.

To compound the issue, population growth is a nonproblem. The worldwide fertility rate has plummeted from 6.5 children per family forty years ago to about 2.5 now, according to Jonathan V. Last, journalist and author of *What to Expect When No One's Expecting: America's Coming Demographic Disaster.* The "replacement rate" for a society to perpetuate itself is a fertility rate of 2.1, as an average of children per woman, while America's current fertility rate is 1.93. This rate is expected to continue to drop.[261] According to the CDC, it has not been above the replacement rate in a sustained way since the early 1970s, about the time of *Roe v. Wade.* And the United States is not alone in this; fertility rates are dropping around the world. Last writes:

> For two generations we've been lectured about the dangers
> of overpopulation. But the conventional wisdom on this
> issue is wrong, twice. First, global population growth is
> slowing to a halt and will begin to shrink within 60 years.
> Second, as the work of economists Esther Boserups and
> Julian Simon demonstrated, growing populations lead

to increased innovation and conservation. Think about it: Since 1970, commodity prices have continued to fall and America's environment has become much cleaner and more sustainable—even though our population has increased by more than 50%. Human ingenuity, it turns out, is the most precious resource.[262]

Still, wealthy individuals and organizations continue to fund measures to control populations, and these "solutions" often victimize women. They, along with the poor and nonwhite people groups, are the typical target of population-control measures. As women are the child bearers, any biological or social changes to enforce population control or eugenic ideas are almost exclusively aimed at them.

The Population Research Institute, a group that seeks to expose the myth of overpopulation, has quantified the impact on women. A PRI-produced list of seventy population-control abuses in thirty countries shows that women have been the targets in sixty-two of the seventy incidents listed. The abuses listed include sterilization, forced abortion, sex-selection abortion, infanticide, or Depo-Provera injections without informed consent.[263]

Sterilization

The recent worldwide history of sterilization shows women are most often the victims. While men have been targeted for sterilization, as in India, where several million men were neutered in the 1970s,[264] women are victimized far more often. The targeting of women and girls to enforce population control is as sad as it is graphic. Sterilization camps in India have been used since the 1970s to reduce India's population growth. A 1994 *Washington Post* report described a camp in Sarsawa,

India, where women were given a local anesthetic and then placed on "makeshift operating tables where a doctor dedicates a total of 45 seconds to each patient—slitting open the belly, inserting a laparoscope, tying the fallopian tubes, dipping the laparoscope into a pail of lukewarm water and then moving on to the next patient."

Afterward, the women were placed in a "dim ward where dozens of women lie side by side on the concrete floor, filling the room with the low moans and quavering wails of excruciating pain." According to the *Washington Post* report, the women "are poor and illiterate, and most are lured to government clinics and camps with promises of houses, land or loans by government officials under intense pressure to meet sterilization quotas."[265]

And this is still going on in India. More than one hundred women were sterilized in one day on February 6, 2013, at a government hospital in West Bengal, India. The postoperative recovery took place in an open field near the sixty-bed hospital, where the women were stretched out on the ground, exposed to the elements and in plain view of hundreds of onlookers.[266]

In Peru, where then-president Alberto Fujimori imposed population-control measures in the late 1990s, Victoria Esperanza Vigo Espinoza was sterilized without her knowledge. She had a C-section, signed a release, and wound up unable to conceive again. "I felt mutilated. That's the truth. My rights as a mother and woman were violated," Vigo said. Hers is not the only case of a Peruvian woman being sterilized without her knowledge. Human rights groups claim there are more than two thousand documented instances of women whose tubes were tied without their knowledge or consent.[267]

Forced sterilization has also taken place right here in the United States. The first law allowing for eugenic sterilizations was passed in

1907 in Indiana, and more than sixty thousand people were sterilized in thirty-three states during the twentieth century.[268] The majority of these were for the purpose of eugenics, following the Supreme Court's 1927 ruling in *Buck v. Bell* that eugenic sterilization was constitutional. Justice Oliver Wendell Holmes Jr. argued that, "to prevent our being swamped with incompetence," "It is better for all the world, if instead of waiting to execute degenerate offspring for crime, or to let them starve for their imbecility, society can prevent those who are manifestly unfit from continuing their kind." Holmes concluded, "Three generations of imbeciles are enough."[269]

Carrie Buck, an eighteen-year-old forcibly sterilized as part of the Court's ruling, was supposedly one of the "three generations of imbeciles," and had been placed into an institution. Ironically, the daughter she had prior to the sterilization (supposedly another "generation of imbeciles") would later be on the honor roll at her school. Historian Paul A. Lombardo has shown that Carrie herself was placed in the institution not due to mental limitations, but in order to hide a rape by her adoptive mother's nephew and save the family shame. Carrie's lawyer was a strong proponent of eugenic sterilization and is suspected to have deliberately argued her case poorly; he was a member of the governing board at the institution holding Carrie and personally signed the sterilization orders.[270]

Buck v. Bell has never been overturned by the Supreme Court, and it was even cited as precedent in the opinion of the Court for *Roe v. Wade* as they considered limitations for abortions. At the Nuremberg trials after World War II, Nazi doctors explicitly cited Justice Holmes's opinion in *Buck v. Bell* as part of their defense.[271]

Countless other women endured similar situations to Carrie Buck's. The documentary *Maafa 21* features an interview with Elaine Riddick, a black woman who was sterilized in 1968 at age fourteen, after she gave birth to a son conceived by rape. She later learned about the operation, which had been approved by the Eugenics Board of North Carolina. She asked "why they did this to me, and they said I was feeble-minded. I would not be able to take care of myself. I would not be able to tie my shoes, that I was just incompetent."

Riddick, a college graduate, said her son is the owner of his own semiconductor, real-estate, and construction firms. She said the state told her "feeble-mindedness was hereditary, so they sterilized me so I would not produce my kind. Mind you, I am not illiterate nor am I feeble-minded. . . . To me, they took away all my rights."[272]

Sterilization laws remained on the books in twenty-seven US states until 1956, but sterilization without consent has retained its presence in the United States up to the twenty-first century. Between 2006 and 2010, 148 female prisoners in two California institutions were sterilized without obtaining their consent.[273]

In Indonesia, there are documented cases of women who had IUDs inserted at gunpoint.[274] In Africa, a University of Nairobi teaching physician relayed "in gory detail how doctors in Kenya routinely cut women's fallopian tubes during cesarean section operations—without even seeking permission to do so in advance."[275]

As we have seen, China practices coercive IUD insertion, sterilization, and abortion. Fines, job loss, and government pressure can be levied against families with more than the allowed number of children. At one house, a husband did not cooperate when authorities told him to have his wife dress and go to the abortion center. So four women on the government team entered the house, struggled with his wife, and then carried her out "in a folded quilt." Two other team members held the husband back when he tried to rescue his wife and preborn child.[276]

Population control and eugenics are obviously not limited to the United States, where forced sterilizations took place long before they were introduced in Nazi Germany or elsewhere. Based on the work of population-control and eugenics groups, these measures occur around the world.

There are two key points from this section:

The victims of population-control and eugenics measures are primarily women. While men (such as the Chinese father mentioned above) suffer emotionally, virtually all physical procedures (sterilization, abortions, and other birth control procedures) are performed on women.

The overwhelming majority of people behind the population-control and eugenics movements historically have been men. This is not to say that women were uninvolved. But almost all of the key players were men in positions of power and wealth.

Population control and eugenics are tools in the hands of powerful men to achieve worldwide control over various populations they deem unworthy to grow. Most of the time, these are minority, handicapped, or impoverished populations.

If you are a person concerned with the care of the poor, you may well be wondering if population control is a valid tool. After all, Margaret Sanger began her journey promoting birth control because of the intense suffering she saw firsthand in impoverished populations. In her mind, educating women on how to limit the number of children was directly connected to their health and welfare.

There is a key point of distinction here, however. Helping the poor to manage the size of their families through proper education is one thing. Knowledge is power, and education is essential for any poor community to rise out of its condition.

However, is it a solution for a powerful population group to impose nonlethal and lethal birth control on other people? Is it right and fair for one group to force another to limit its population?

Here's why the questions are essential. The logical conclusion to discriminatory birth control is always abortion. As eugenicists in the 1900s discovered, education wasn't enough. Sterilization was the next step, and, if that didn't work, the only final solution was abortion.

In the case of America, it was powerful, rich, white men who were behind the legalization of abortion, not women.

But men have another reason to push abortion, and it has nothing to do with worldwide population control or racism.

CHAPTER 7
"I'll Still Love You in the Morning"

As this review of world history has revealed, men have a habit of using women for their sexual pleasure. Whether through the practices of binding feet, harems, or prostitution; the legal ease of getting a divorce (so a new wife can be acquired); or pornography, men in numerous cultures throughout world history have used their power, money, and influence to satisfy their sexual urges outside of a relationship or environment that is equally beneficial for women.

Obviously, pregnancy is a natural and normal outcome of sexual relations, whether those relations are for one gender's benefit or both.

Throughout the course of American history, unintended pregnancies have been dealt with in a number of ways. Quick "shotgun" weddings were an option, where the father and mother married in haste in order to avoid the once-public shame of an unintended pregnancy.

Sending the woman away for several months was another option. The woman would disappear for a time (perhaps with an excuse of visiting a relative or going to boarding school), give birth to the child, and then return home. The public embarrassment was still prevalent, but the woman didn't have to bear public scorn while pregnant.

Prior to 1973, illegal abortion was also an option.

The Other American Revolution

As the sexual revolution of the 1960s exploded and traditional marriage began to erode, men broke the boundaries of sexual control. Abstinence before marriage started to become a public joke, and the concepts of living together and no-fault divorce began to gain public acceptance.

While the sexual revolution is normally associated with the '60s, its actual launch can be dated to 1948, when Indiana University researcher Alfred Kinsey released *Sexual Behavior in the Human Male*, with funding assistance from the Rockefeller Foundation. The best-selling report purported to show that nearly all American men were sexual adventurers who routinely flouted the bounds of marriage. Widely publicized as the verdict of sober science, Kinsey's research claimed that 85 percent of men had sex before marriage and 70 percent used prostitutes. Between 30 and 45 percent of married men had affairs, and 10 to 37 percent of men engaged in homosexual encounters.[277]

Kinsey is credited as the "Father of the Sexual Revolution" for his work, but his research was junk science. Even aside from being sexually aberrant in his personal life—including self-circumcision with a pocket knife—and likely allowing his own preferences to influence his studies,[278] Kinsey's findings were still unreliable. Dr. Judith Reisman has revealed that Kinsey and his researchers "based their claims about normal males on a roughly 86 percent aberrant male population including 200 sexual psychopaths, 1,400 sex offenders and hundreds each of prisoners, male prostitutes, and promiscuous homosexuals."[279] His "findings" on "normal females" were based on similarly dubious samples. Other scientists and researchers came out in droves to poke holes in Kinsey's methods; the list of his critics, Kinsey biographer James H. Jones observes, "read like a Who's Who of American Intellectual Life." Anthropologist Geoffrey Gorer summed up the scientific community's reaction when he called Kinsey's reports "propaganda masquerading as science."[280] The Rockefeller Foundation even withdrew its funding. In the years since, no reputable scientific survey has ever been able to duplicate Kinsey's findings—because they were ludicrously faulty to begin with.

And yet Kinsey was at least partly responsible for a cultural shift that loosened America's sexual mores, one that supposedly gave scientific license to entire generations to follow their impulses because it was normal and natural. Kinsey also inspired *Playboy* publisher Hugh Hefner, that famous advocate of unlimited sexual gratification. Hefner, who founded *Playboy* in 1953, considered himself Kinsey's "pamphleteer, spreading the news of sexual liberation through a monthly magazine."[281] Hefner also worked to legalize abortion through his Playboy Foundation, established in 1965. "We fought for birth control rights and the change in birth control laws, the change in abortion laws, we fought cases to give women the right to choose," Hefner has said.[282]

His magazine came out for abortion's legalization in 1965 and, in 1967, encouraged readers to call legislators in those states then considering a relaxation of legal limits on abortion. The magazine covered abortion law developments and publicized abortion services, providing phone numbers, costs, and other information.[283]

Women, Hefner claims, have been the "major beneficiaries of the sexual revolution." What it achieved, he said, "was give freedom to both sexes not only in the bedroom, but everywhere else."[284]

No-fault divorce was another alleged benefit to both men and women that arrived about the same time as the sexual revolution. California governor Ronald Reagan signed the nation's first no-fault divorce bill into law in 1969, and the rest of the states followed over the next fifteen years. According to Reagan's son Michael, signing this bill was his father's "greatest regret" of his public service.[285] No-fault divorce laws allow one spouse to leave the marriage without evidence of adultery or abandonment by simply claiming discontent based on vague complaints like "mental cruelty" or "incompatibility."

The result has been disastrous. The divorce rate per 1,000 married women in the United States more than doubled between 1960 and 1980, jumping from 9.2 to 22.6,[286] as no-fault divorce laws took effect across the nation. Political scientist Stephen Baskerville says easy divorce is the "most direct threat to the family" and says it must be resolved "if civilization is to endure."[287]

Fortified by the "findings" of Kinsey, inflamed with the *Playboy* philosophy, and given an easy "out" by abortion and no-fault divorce, men have, for the last generation, pursued sexual gratification with reckless abandon. And I do mean reckless:

The number of couples living together outside marriage jumped seventeenfold from 1960 to 2010.[288]

Nearly 22 percent of men ages fifteen to forty-five have had fifteen or more sex partners.[289]

The illegitimacy rate is now almost 41 percent.[290]

There are an estimated 20 million new sexually transmitted infections annually.[291]

To be sure, women have participated in the process. But, as with the social agendas related to abortion, men have orchestrated the movement and led the charge.

The "problem" with sexual freedom outside marriage is pregnancy. Inside marriage, pregnancy is generally accepted and desired. Outside of marriage, pregnancy is often an unintended consequence of sexual freedom and thus poses a threat to that freedom.

So what do men do when their sexual freedom causes a pregnancy? That pregnancy, which under all normal circumstances results in the birth of a child, brings a whole new set of responsibilities and commitments. As any parent knows, a child brings an enormous amount of change to any family, along with numerous obligations, which weren't present prior to the pregnancy.

Just a Theory, Mind You

Allow me to propose a theory. What if pregnancy could be terminated so that sexual freedom could be maintained? And what if men had no responsibility for the pregnancy or its termination? And, in the best of all scenarios, what if women actually celebrated the responsibility for pregnancy and its termination and gave men no credit, no right, and no voice in that process?

Abortion is the ultimate "get out of jail free" card for sexually aggressive men. Men can continue having sexual relations with multiple women, refuse to commit to any one woman in marriage, and divorce a woman through no-fault divorce if they aren't sexually or emotionally satisfied. And if, along the way, a woman gets pregnant, the man has avoided all responsibility to that woman for his child. Maybe they cough up a few hundred bucks for the abortion; maybe not.

Is this just a theory? Surely men wouldn't be so crass, so manipulative, so selfish that they would intentionally use abortion as a way of pursuing their sexual appetites. They wouldn't so easily cast their female partners aside, leaving them to deal with the impact of pregnancy or the typical devastation of abortion. They certainly wouldn't abandon their female partners just because their sex life led to a pregnancy.

Sadly, even our quick review of men's historical—and contemporary—treatment of women around the globe makes this scenario not simply possible, but likely.

Is this the path to elevating the role of women in society?

Ironically, numerous scholars and sociologists readily admit abortion is all about sex. And they candidly confess abortion is really about men having the freedom to do what they want with no consequence.

Catharine MacKinnon, an influential feminist legal scholar, writes that abortion "does not liberate women; it frees male sexual aggression. The availability of abortion removes the one remaining legitimized reason that women have had for refusing sex besides the headache."[292]

And that is why, she notes, "the Playboy Foundation has supported abortion rights from day one" at a level on par with its other *cause célèbre*, "opposition to censorship." As another feminist writer, Andrea Dworkin, put it much more crassly, "Getting laid was at stake."[293] Or as an abortion advocate said at a UN conference, "Let's stop fooling around here. What we're talking about is our right to f*** whoever we want, however we want, whenever we want."[294]

Feminist Dorchen Leidholdt sees it pretty much the same but puts it more politely:

> Sexually liberal men support abortion for women not because they want women to be able to control their bodies but because they know that unrestricted abortions heighten women's availability to men for sex.[295]

The most astonishing thing about all this is that, despite feminist rhetoric about rights and empowerment, abortion deeply wounds women and gives men license to exploit them. Some feminists do understand this.

In recent years, a few have recognized the sheer injustice of asking a woman to abort her child in order to participate fully in society. In the words of the New Zealand feminist author Daphne de Jong: "If women must submit to abortion to preserve their lifestyle or career, their economic or social status, they are pandering to a system devised and run by men for male convenience."[296]

More evidence for this sexual agenda comes from an unwitting source, the Center for Reproductive Rights, which produced a video meant to celebrate *Roe*'s fortieth anniversary. Instead, the quickly-pulled piece was a painful self-parody displaying the truth behind abortion rights. The CRR production featured a black actor dressed in a suit before a fireplace, with a glass of liquor and a rose on the table in front of him. He chuckles, leers, and says, as if speaking to *Roe*, "Happy anniversary, baby. Looking good for forty," his voice trailing off in a series of grunts that close with a contented sigh.

This crude video reveals, once more, that male sexual appetite is a primary driver of the abortion rights movement in America.

These examples and quotes are not from life-affirming or family organizations. With the exception of Daphne de Jong, they are from abortion advocates, feminists, and one of the most vocal organizations promoting abortion in America. Beneath the marketing campaigns that promote "choice," "reproductive rights," and "empowering women" lies the real social reason for abortion: men having the freedom to sleep with whoever they want with no legal or social consequence to themselves.

This has been the underlying social reason for abortion for centuries.

Writing in 1871, Dr. John Cowan listed the "licentiousness of the man and the bondage of the woman" as the cause of the "monstrous crime . . . the murder of the unborn."[297]

129

Another nineteenth-century doctor summed up the role of sexually liberal men well. Acknowledging that abortion oppresses women, Dr. John Trader argued that the impetus and responsibility for abortion rests with men: "We do not affirm, neither would we have you think for a moment, that the onus of this guilt lies at the feet of women. Far from it. In the majority of cases, they are more sinned against than sinning."[298]

And, as noted earlier, feminist Susan B. Anthony wrote:

> I deplore the horrible crime of child-murder. . . . No matter what the motive, love or ease, or a desire to save from suffering the unborn innocent, the woman is awfully guilty who commits the deed, but, oh! thrice guilty is he who drove her to the desperation which impelled her to the crime.[299]

CHAPTER 8
Educated Choice?

At this point, you may be thinking, "So what? So what if men have primarily controlled the promotion and legalization of abortion? Even if men are the 'wizards behind the curtain,' they have still advanced female rights. Women still have the right to choose, and, for that, we are grateful to men."

But do women really have that right? Do they have complete freedom to choose abortion or not? Do women get all the facts, medically and emotionally speaking, to make an informed decision? Are they able to independently make that choice, free from the influence and coercion of men?

Sadly, the answer is clearly no. Though it is a woman's right to choose whether or not to abort, the data once again show that men continue to have tremendous influence over that decision. Male coercion, whether active or passive, plays a huge role in the abortion decision.

Informed?

If women are to be fully empowered, they must be educated. Women have fought for this right in various cultures for good reason. Making decisions from ignorance can have dire consequences.

In America, we strive for female education and equality. Women generally have the same opportunities as men for public or private schooling, collegiate and postgraduate education.

In matters of health, America strongly encourages women to be fully educated about their bodies, how to fight illnesses, how to take care of themselves, and how to protect and defend themselves.

We encourage patients, male and female, to seek second opinions when diagnosed with an illness or injury that requires extensive care. In regard to female health, the medical community seeks to provide mammograms, PAP smears, and numerous other female examinations in order to inform about and protect women from potentially harmful health issues.

Do we provide the same sort of commitment, education, and re-dundancy when a woman is faced with the decision of whether or not to willfully take the life of another human being? Do we fully disclose to women that the decision to abort very often comes with extremely difficult emotional and physical side effects?

It's one thing to educate women about breast cancer screenings. We all consider this to be vital and necessary. Do we not think that a full education is required if the decision has a life-and-death impact on another human being?

Apparently not.

The Elliot Institute cites research showing that information and counseling are in short supply for women contemplating an abortion. According to these findings,[300] among women considering abortion:

54 percent were unsure of their decision, yet 67 percent received no counseling beforehand;

84 percent were inadequately counseled beforehand;

79 percent were deceived or not told about available resources; and

many were misinformed by experts about fetal development, abortion alternatives, or risks.

The Elliot Institute also reports that many postabortive women say they were denied essential personal, family, societal, or economic support. One study, for example, found that 64 percent of women who had an abortion said their partner did not provide support.[301]

Theresa Burke, the founder of Rachel's Vineyard, a ministry that helps men and women find healing after abortion, says the lack of support continues after abortion. While nearly 78 percent of postabortive women report feeling guilty,[302] the therapeutic safety net is nonexistent. There is little in the way of acknowledgement, let alone support.

"The psychological and spiritual agony of abortion is silenced by society, ignored by the media, rebuffed by mental health professionals, and scorned by the women's movement," says Burke. "Post-abortion trauma is a serious and devastating illness which has no celebrity spokeswoman, no made-for-television movie, and no platform for the talk show confessional."[303]

And are women fully educated on the severe risks associated with abortion?

> Women who have abortions are nearly four times more likely to die later from accident-related injuries.[304] One study found that women who had abortions had a 62 percent higher risk of death from all causes than did women who gave birth. Factors leading to death included suicide and accidents.[305]
>
> Suicide rates are six times higher after abortion.[306]
>
> 65 percent of women suffer trauma symptoms after abortion.[307]

And while we are discussing informed consent, we should consider the Planned Parenthood videos that surfaced in 2015, which revealed that women were not being informed that their aborted babies' body parts were being sold. The undercover videos, released by the Center for Medical Progress, caused an initial firestorm in the mass media and a backlash from abortion advocates. Although this story is too big to fully cover here, it's important to note that not only were women not being adequately informed about the trade in fetal remains, but the enforced ignorance continued with the media's one-sided coverage of the videos.

Planned Parenthood commissioned and funded a review of the videos, carried out by a group with ties to the Democratic party,[308] which found them to be "edited" and prompted countless journalists and others to accuse CMP of manipulation and to dismiss their claims outright. A second report was then carried out by an independent, third-party, internationally respected digital and forensic firm that does work for Fortune 500 companies and analyzes evidence in civil and criminal investigations. This firm had access to the full, raw footage and found it to be "authentic" with "no evidence of manipulation"; the released videos had only been edited, the report stated, to omit "non-pertinent" footage such as bathroom breaks.[309] The firm provided specific details and screenshots to support their findings, and the report was sent to every major media outlet in the country.[310]

They all promptly ignored it. There was no response in the mainstream media to this report, an independent finding that should have prompted the same furor of articles and editorials as the Planned Parenthood-funded report. Instead, silence, as if it had never existed.

Meanwhile, CMP founder David Daleiden has faced charges and intense pressure to cease his exposure of Planned Parenthood.

In April 2016, his home was raided and personal property seized, including additional evidence, under the direction of California Attorney General Kamala Harris, who is a US Senate candidate with a campaign funded by, you guessed it, Planned Parenthood.[311] There is no "shield law" protecting abortionists from investigative journalism, and other undercover activists have sought to expose SeaWorld, the meatpacking industry, and others, with no mass condemnation from the media or retribution from political figures. The attacks on Daleiden and any findings that support his cause are selective and political.

The suppression of information that is of direct, overwhelmingly pertinent impact to ongoing investigations and a major public issue is inexcusable. People cannot make informed choices unless they are given both sides of the story.

In the same way, women cannot make educated decisions about their health and their pregnancies unless they are given all of the information, not a heavily skewed version of one part of it.

Independent?

If we are concerned about women's equality and rights, we should not only be concerned about women being properly informed about abortion, we should also be concerned about their ability to make an abortion decision independent of male coercion.

While the majority of women are not properly informed of their options and, therefore, are often making a life-and-death decision (one that impacts their personal and mental health greatly) without all of the facts, surely women are able to make the decision without male interference? After all, that is true gender equality, is it not?

Once again, women are exploited by men.

64 percent of women reported feeling pressured to abort.[312]

Most felt rushed or uncertain, yet 67 percent weren't counseled.[313]

Clinics fail to screen for coercion.[314]

Many times the pressure to abort comes from a male figure, generally the father of the baby or the woman's father. And the pressure is not just emotional.

Pressure to abort can escalate to violence.[315]

There are numerous examples of this coercion:[316]

> He destroyed our apartment . . . and told me to get rid of it. Now! The whole time he cornered me . . . throwing things and killing me with his words. The abortion ripped me apart. Any strength I had to leave the abuse was torn away from me.
>
> —Mary

> I was a victim of incest at fifteen. . . . In spite of the pain and guilt I felt, it was far better to have a baby than the alternative—to kill it. I refused to have an abortion. . . . My father flew into an uncontrollable rage and demanded that I consent to the abortion. . . . [The doctor] asked three nurses to hold me while he strapped me to the bed. . . . I continued to scream that I didn't want an abortion. He told me, "Shut up and quit that yelling!" . . . I was violated by my father . . . I was violated again by the abortionist.
>
> —Denise (not real name)

> No one would support me. . . . The worst day of my life got closer and closer. . . . I think in more cases than

not, it isn't the woman's choice. It should be called "Your Parents' and the Guy's Choice.". . . I needed someone to tell me that it was possible to keep my baby, but no one did. . . ."

—Amanda

Sometimes the coercion is active and violent. Pregnant women are already at much higher risk of inflicted harm; studies have shown that homicide is the leading cause of death for pregnant women in the United States,[317] while for American females as a whole it does not even rank in the top ten.[318] Many times, it is the father's passive approach or simple unwillingness to parent that overpowers a woman's desire to nurture and protect her child.

The Guttmacher Institute, a proabortion research organization that was originally a branch of Planned Parenthood, conducted a study of twenty-one postabortive women who experienced difficulty, including a sense of regret, after the abortion. The study reported that "negative outcomes" followed when the father took a pass on his responsibility for the pregnancy and left the mother "feeling as though she had no other choice."[319]

Another study indicates that the most important factor in a woman's decision to abort a second pregnancy is, rather than poverty, whether the father has been active or passive in the care of a first child. The likelihood of abortion rose significantly, the study found, when women felt that the father was unlikely to "watch the child for a week," "take good care of the child," "watch the child when the mother needs to do things," or if he "does not support the mother's way of raising the child" and "does not respect the schedule and rules" the child is to follow.[320] And, no surprise, the study, published in the *International Journal of*

Mental Health and Addiction, also found that marriage made abortion much less likely.[321]

Agreeable fathers who say, "Sure, babe, I'll support your abortion decision, if that's what you want," may see the relationship turn cold and angry afterward, says researcher Dr. Vincent Rue. "One of the sad realities of abortion," he writes, "is how caring men, who try not to hurt the women they love, in fact hurt them by saying nothing when abortion is first mentioned in the crisis decision-making process."

Men who are passive and compliant toward their abortion-minded mate may wind up facing "a fierce, often denied, undercurrent of resentment stemming from their partner's feelings of abandonment," according to Dr. Rue, who is codirector of the Institute for Pregnancy Loss in Jacksonville, Florida. "Wanting to please, these men are rejected because they were judged deficient in true love for their partners."[322]

That "undercurrent of resentment" surfaced at the Red River Women's Clinic, a Fargo, North Dakota, abortion facility. It's a place, according to a *Time* magazine report, where female patients, who are encouraged to express their feelings in journals, "write about nonsupportive husbands and boyfriends and ask God for forgiveness."[323]

Is abortion empowering for women? If they are not fully informed about the risks and potential side effects of abortion, and if they are heavily influenced by males in the abortion decision, just how empowering is it?

Intelligent?

Ironically, it seems like some in our culture think women are too stupid to make an informed decision. They don't want women getting a second opinion from a source that doesn't support abortion.

One woman, commenting on the Human Coalition iPhone app mentioned previously, wrote:

> Nothing but judgmental and manipulative means to brainwash woman [*sic*] by standing behind the cliché catch phrase of "providing options." Using sonogram propaganda to guilt women into "saving a life" further confirms the stupidity of ignorant Bible thumping leaders who continue to take your money so they can create absurd Apps such as these. Keep those prayers coming folks. I'm sure your [*sic*] saving those babies [*sic*] lives.

In 2013, a news story aired about the twenty-four-hour mandatory waiting period for abortion in my home state of Texas. A proabortion state politician complained about the waiting period, claiming it was harmful to women, caused confusion, and put more pressure on women when they have already made up their minds. She said the law runs the risk of manipulating women's minds.

This sentiment is common. Women should not get separate counsel and not have to wait a day or two to consider other options. They are supposedly susceptible to brainwashing and can't make an informed decision. They are too easily manipulated to be able to handle opinions contrary to the abortion provider's.

If a woman is about to have a surgical procedure, do we not want her to have information about all alternatives? Should she not be informed about the possible outcomes of all options? I would think so. We want her to know about the pre-op, post-op, and recovery expectations. We want her to know if there are any holistic or alternative medicines that could assist her. Perhaps her surgery could be avoided with proper diet, exercise, or vitamins. We would all feel a strong commitment to making sure the woman has the opportunity to see her potential surgery and its alternatives from all angles, so she can make the best decision for herself.

And, in the case of abortion, the surgery ends the life of another human being. Not only are we considering the life and well-being of the mother, but abortion is a life-and-death decision.

Are women so susceptible to manipulation and brainwashing that they can't sort through the information to make an informed decision?

Apparently women aren't very intelligent, discerning, or wise.

So, are the majority of women properly educated when considering abortion? The data points to a severe lack of appropriate information and counsel.

Are the majority of women making independent decisions regarding abortion? No. In the majority of cases, they are heavily influenced or coerced by others—namely, men.

Are women capable of handling a variety of viewpoints about their abortion decision? Apparently not, as many think they are too dumb or weak to think through contrary viewpoints about abortion, a surgery that verifiably ends the life of another human being.

CHAPTER 9
It's "Safe" and "Rare"?

I t's one thing to read the book thus far and disregard the facts. It may not bother you that men are primarily responsible for the rise and legalization of abortion in America. It may not bother you that abortion is a tool in the hands of eugenicists and population-control advocates. And it may not even bother you to concede that sexually active males use abortion as a "get out of jail free" card, even though women are left to deal with the pregnancy, the surgical or chemical abortion procedure, and the aftermath of abortion.

After all, abortion is a woman's right. Who can tell a woman what to do with her body?

If you refuse to concede that abortion is a means for men to exploit women for their own gain and instead choose to celebrate the right to abort, then you'll need to come to grips with the effects of abortion on women. You are celebrating a right that does tremendous emotional and physical damage to the female gender.

To understand the impact of abortion on women, let's take a look at how and why women abort. Though we often hear about abortion being used in cases of rape and incest, the overwhelming majority of cases are for very different reasons.

Birth Control

Abortion is the final form of birth control in America. It's used as such for several reasons—primarily because contraceptives are routinely ineffective or, perhaps more likely, Americans aren't using them properly and with regularity. People may claim they use contraception, but that doesn't mean they use it as designed and every time they have sex.

Abortion proponents often get upset when I link abortion to birth control, but it isn't actually my conclusion. According to a 2012 CDC report, 89 percent of American women at risk of unintended pregnancy—that is, sexually active and physically capable of bearing children—use contraceptives. Nearly all sexually experienced women (99.1 percent) have used contraception at some point.[324] However, contraception isn't working too well. The CDC reports that nearly one-half (49 percent) of all pregnancies in the United States are unintended.

If we do the math, and consider that there are over 5.2 million pregnancies each year, this means that, by a conservative estimate, contraception (whether because of a faulty product or a faulty user) is failing over 2 million times each year.

And the success rate of contraception hasn't been improving. The US Department of Health and Human Services reports the average probability of an unintended pregnancy in twelve months of contraceptive use in the United States is 12 percent. That number hasn't moved since 1995.[325]

Guttmacher Institute researchers Lawrence Finer and Mia Zolna report, "Nearly half of pregnancies among American women are unintended, and about four in 10 of these are terminated by abortion."[326] If contraceptives are failing over 2 million times a year, and nearly half of those unintended pregnancies are ending in abortion, abortion is being used as a final form of birth control.

Proabortion advocates get upset because they think this implies that women are unfeeling. They maintain that women wrestle with the decision to abort. I'm not claiming that abortion isn't a hard decision or that women who abort are somehow callous and unfeeling.

I am saying the data doesn't lie.

Fully 75 percent of women having abortions offer convenience-related reasons for doing so. If we carefully review Guttmacher's statements below, we see abortion is a means of birth control:

> The reasons women give for having an abortion underscore their understanding of the responsibilities of parenthood and family life. Three-fourths of women cite concern for or responsibility to other individuals; three-fourths say they cannot afford a child; three-fourths say that having a baby would interfere with work, school or the ability to care for dependents; and half say they do not want to be a single parent or are having problems with their husband or partner.[327]

If we wade through the spin in that paragraph, we note that the primary reasons listed are finances, interference with work or other responsibilities, or issues with the father of the baby. In fact, the primary reasons given may well be the same reasons we would use for preventative contraception.

In a debate, Ann Furedi, the chief executive of BPAS, Britain's largest abortion provider, said, "In the real world, out of women who are using the pill well, about 8 in every 100 will get pregnant in the course of a year. . . . We need abortion as a backup to contraception."[328]

And that is exactly what abortion is in America today. The backup to, and final form of, birth control.

So is this form of birth control safe for women? Do they suffer any ill effects that should be known and disclosed? How about other family members—do they experience any negative impact when an abortion is performed?

Harmful Effects On Women: Death

If abortion is being used primarily as birth control, then is it also saving their lives? Or, if we are going to talk about the harmful effects of abortion on women, is death a primary risk?

It is worth remembering that the original push for the legalization of abortion was to make sure the procedure was safe for women. Our nation was concerned about women's health and wanted to stop back-alley abortions. So, in order to make sure abortion would be "safe" and "rare," it was legalized.

However there weren't enough deaths of mothers by abortion to legitimize the claim that abortion had to be made legal. So facts were fabricated.

Bernard Nathanson wrote, "There were perhaps three hundred or so deaths from criminal abortions annually in the United States in the sixties, but NARAL in its press releases claimed to have data that supported a figure of five thousand."[329]

The claim of 8,000 to 10,000 abortion-related maternal deaths annually was first introduced in 1936 by abortion-legalization advocate Dr. Frederick Taussig, who later acknowledged those numbers were based on "the wildest estimates."[330] Dr. Christopher Tietze, an abortion legalization advocate who served as a statistician for Planned Parenthood, dismissed the exaggerated numbers in a 1969 *Scientific American* article:

Some 30 years ago it was judged that such deaths [from illegal abortion] might number 5,000 to 10,000 per year, but this rate even if it was approximately correct at the time, cannot be anywhere near the true rate now. The total number of deaths from all causes among women of reproductive age in the U.S. is not more than about 50,000 per year. The National Center for Health Statistics listed 235 deaths from abortion in 1965. Total mortality from illegal abortions was undoubtedly larger than that figure, but in all likelihood it was under 1,000.[331]

Others had presumed that abortion was not immediately physically dangerous to women. Dr. Mary Calderone, then medical director of Planned Parenthood, wrote an article in 1960 for the *American Journal of Public Health*, stating, "Abortion, whether therapeutic or illegal, is in the main no longer dangerous, because it is being done well by physicians."[332]

Her conclusion was not just her own. She was citing the judgment reached by forty-three medical professionals, who gathered together in a series of eight three-hour sessions to "exhaustively" address the issue of illegal abortion. According to Calderone, citing the conference of professionals:

Abortion is no longer a dangerous procedure. This applies not just to therapeutic abortions as performed in hospitals but also to so-called illegal abortions as done by physicians. In 1957 there were only 260 deaths in the whole country attributed to abortions of any kind.[333]

This number of abortion deaths had plummeted by 1972 when, according to the CDC, there were thirty-nine maternal deaths due to illegal abortion and twenty-four deaths due to legal abortion.[334] That's an 85 percent decline in the fifteen years between 1957 and 1972.

So, in 1972 there were a reported sixty-three deaths due to botched abortions—legal or illegal. While these deaths are tragic, exponentially more people are killed in traffic accidents each year. In 2014, ninety-three people died on roads in America *every day*.[335]

Even though the reported number of maternal deaths by abortion was fabricated, and the number of deaths remains small, it is still a viable risk.

A twenty-four-year-old woman died after a Chicago Planned Parenthood abortionist botched the abortion of her sixteen-week-old baby on July 20, 2012. The woman suffered severe bleeding from the incomplete abortion but was not transported to a hospital for five and a half hours. The autopsy report indicates fetal parts left behind by Planned Parenthood, a three-sixteenths-inch uterine perforation, and an "extensive" perforation, which may have severed an artery and caused massive internal bleeding. There were one to one and a half liters of blood in her abdominal cavity, indicating she lost up to 30 percent of her total blood supply.[336]

Another woman died in Maryland on February 7, 2013, after she sought an abortion at thirty-three weeks from late-term abortionist Dr. LeRoy Carhart. Jennifer Morbelli, a twenty-nine-year-old married kindergarten teacher, first arrived at the Germantown Reproductive Health Center in Germantown, Maryland, on Sunday, February 3. According to a report from Operation Rescue,

> she was seen by pro-life activists [outside the abortion facility] every day through Wednesday. Witnesses

146

said she appeared "pale and weak." Early Thursday morning, the woman began suffering chest pain and other discomforts. Her attempts to reach Carhart were unsuccessful. The woman was taken by her family from her hotel to a nearby hospital emergency room at approximately 5:00 a.m. Efforts by hospital staff to contact Carhart or get informational assistance from the abortion clinic were unsuccessful.

The patient suffered massive internal bleeding into her abdominal cavity. She slipped into a Code Blue condition approximately six times before finally succumbing to her injuries at around 9:30 a.m. The case has been placed with the Medical Examiner for further investigation.[337]

And, as noted above, the leading cause of death for pregnant women is murder. The risk to the mother and child is not just in the abortion clinic; it extends in some cases to a violent male in the mother's life who does not wish her to have the baby. This pressure may push her to abort the developing child, an action with its own life-and-death consequences.

Botched Abortions

Botched abortions and cruel abortionists can be brutally harmful to women.

Former Philadelphia abortionist Kermit Gosnell, who was convicted for murder in the deaths of infants aborted alive and killed by a scissor snip to their spinal columns, treated his patients with contempt and cruelty. When Davida Johnson changed her mind, he forced her to have an abortion anyway. "I said, 'I don't want to do this,' and he smacked me," Johnson told the Associated Press. "They tied my hands and arms down and gave me more medication."[338]

Another woman was left unattended for hours after Gosnell cut both her cervix and colon in an unsuccessful attempt to remove her baby. Relatives of the woman, who were at first refused entry into Gosnell's clinic, later found her dazed and bleeding and took her to a hospital, where doctors removed a half-foot of her intestine.[339]

A forty-year-old woman is suing a Colorado Planned Parenthood office after the abortionist there forced her to undergo an abortion without anesthesia and left parts of her baby's dismembered body inside her uterus. The woman, who had to be treated in an emergency room, alleges in her lawsuit that she changed her mind while on the operating table because the agreed-upon anesthesia was not administered due to difficulty inserting an IV into her vein. The abortionist told her it was too late to change her mind and flipped on the vacuum machine to do the abortion, forcing her to endure the full pain of the seven-minute procedure.[340]

A Michigan woman had to be rushed by ambulance to a hospital in 2009 to stop uncontrolled bleeding six months after her abortion. "If my boyfriend hadn't woken me up that night, I just feel like I could have bled to death in my sleep," said the woman, who was given two units of blood and an emergency D&C. The woman recalled "being in a lot of pain" during the abortion procedure and said she visited the clinic's bathroom after the abortion, where she saw "blood all over the restroom, including on the toilet seat."[341] The local fire department shut down the clinic on December 27, 2012, one day after discovering conditions "dangerous to human life or the public welfare." An inspection revealed, for example, "blood dripping from a sink p-trap in a room used by patients."[342]

Mark Crutcher lists these examples of how women suffer at the hands of abusive abortionists in his exposé of the abortion industry, *Lime 5: Exploited by Choice*:

> In response to a woman's screams of pain during her abortion, a clinic worker stuffed a tampon in her mouth. During the procedure, she was so badly injured that she lost all of her reproductive organs and spleen and ended up with a colostomy, as well as permanent damage to her heart, lungs, and kidneys.

> An abortionist showed a 12-week-old fetus that he had just aborted to the patient, threw his glove on the floor, and asked her if she was "satisfied."

> A woman claimed that her abortionist "ordered [her] on the table and threw her legs apart." She said she felt like she was some animal at which the doctor was irritated.[343]

Other Physical Effects

Other increased physical risks to the mother include cervical, ovarian, and liver cancers; uterine perforations; cervical lacerations; preterm deliveries and other labor complications; and pelvic inflammatory disease, or PID, an infection of the uterus that can damage the Fallopian tubes.[344]

Another physical risk garnering debate in the media is the increased risk of breast cancer after an abortion. Despite denying a link between abortion and breast cancer, a 2009 study published in the journal *Cancer Epidemiology, Biomarkers and Prevention* found:

... examined risk factors were consistent with the effects of previous studies on younger women. Specifically, older age, family history of breast cancer, earlier menarche age, *induced abortion*, and oral contraceptives were associated with an increased risk of breast cancer.[345]

More recently, Dr. Angela Lanfranchi, president of the Breast Cancer Prevention Institute, reported at a National Press Club media briefing that "there are 70 published studies examining the risk of induced abortion and breast cancer of which 55 show a positive correlation and 33 are statistically significant."[346] According to Lanfranchi, "The overwhelming evidence from worldwide epidemiologic studies shows that abortion is a cause for breast cancer."[347]

Impact on Subsequent Children

Abortion also presents potential risks to subsequent children who are not aborted.

Dr. Freda McKissic Bush, an obstetrician-gynecologist and president/CEO of the Medical Institute for Sexual Health, states, "Abortion greatly increases a woman's chance of giving birth prematurely in the next pregnancy."[348] The rate of prematurity, which is the leading cause of infant death in the United States, has doubled since the legalization of abortion, Dr. Bush reports, rising from six percent before 1970 to 12.8 percent in 2006 and currently at 11.7 percent.

Prematurity is a problem that disproportionately impacts African American women, says Dr. Bush. Black women have premature babies, before thirty-two weeks gestation, at three times the rate of white women. This fact points to abortion, since black women have 35 percent of all abortions but blacks make up just 13 percent of the population.

"There are over 130 studies in the medical literature showing that abortion leads to an increase in very premature births (births before 8 months of pregnancy)," according to Dr. Bush. "Those preemie babies are the ones who end up with cerebral palsy, developmental problems and mental impairments."[349]

A Finnish study found an increased risk of preterm birth after abortion and reported that the risk increases with two or more abortions. Dr. Reija Klemetti, who led the research, said that "for every 1000 women, three who have had no abortion will have a baby born under 28 weeks. . . . This rises to four women among those who have had one abortion, six women who have had two abortions, and 11 women who have had three or more."[350]

Abortion activist and NARAL cofounder Lawrence Lader believed abortion would ultimately be beneficial to society. Writing in *The Humanist* magazine, Lader predicted the positive effects of abortion:

> The impact of the abortion revolution may be too vast to assess immediately. It should usher in an era when every child will be wanted, loved, and properly cared for; when the incidence of infanticides and battered children should be sharply reduced.[351]

Yet violence breeds violence. One violent act of abortion (which may or may not be preceded by other violence) can now be connected to higher incidences of further violence.

A 2005 study led by Dr. Priscilla Coleman found, "Compared to women with no history of induced abortion, those with one prior abortion had a 144 percent higher risk for child physical abuse."[352] Dr. Michael J. New, an assistant professor at the University of Michigan-Dearborn, cites data from the US Statistical Abstract showing that child abuse increased by 400 percent between 1973 and 1990.[353] Between 1970 and 1990, the abortion ratio in America similarly exploded, increasing 645 percent.[354]

Abortion advocates claim that wanted children will be welcomed and loved while those born from unplanned pregnancies are more likely to suffer abuse, but empirical research contradicts that view. A 1980 study of 674 abused children conducted by researcher Edward Lenoski found that 91 percent of the abused children in the study were wanted by their parents.[355] What makes this striking is that just half of all pregnancies in the United States are planned, according to the Guttmacher Institute. This means that abused children are disproportionately from families where the parents wanted and planned for them.

The logic of abortion—which makes preborn children expendable and subject to death—also puts born children at risk. Psychiatrist Philip Ney suggests the following seven mechanisms explain why abortion makes child abuse more likely:

> Abortion decreases an individual's instinctual restraint against the occasional rage felt toward those dependent on his or her care.
>
> Permissive abortion diminishes the taboo against aggressing [against] the defenseless.
>
> Abortion increases the hostility between the generations.
>
> Abortion has devalued children, thus diminishing the value of caring for children.
>
> Abortion increases guilt and self-hatred, which the parent takes out on the child.

> Abortion increases hostile frustration, intensi-
> fying the battle of the sexes, for which children are
> scapegoated.
>
> Abortion truncates the developing mother-infant
> bond, thereby diminishing her future mothering capa-
> bility.[356, 357]

Instead of incidences of battered children being sharply reduced, as Lader predicted, abortion has brought further violence to children both inside and outside the womb.

Psychological Impacts

Novelist Erica Jong supports abortion but is candid about its emotional toll. This author of provocative, sexual novels writes that abortion, for her, was too high a price to pay:

> As a seventeen-year-old freshman at Barnard, I got my
> first diaphragm from Planned Parenthood (a college
> tradition). I never got pregnant accidentally because I
> knew that an abortion would make me terribly sad. I
> loved children, dogs, cats and other living things, and
> I understood that terminating a pregnancy would be
> extremely hard for me emotionally.[358]

Research confirms what Jong understood: the mental health consequences of abortion are enormous. A 1997 Finnish study found, according to a review of its results, that "women who abort are approximately four times more likely to die in the following year than women who carry their pregnancies to term."[359] Relative to women who did give birth, women who aborted a year prior to their death were:

seven times more likely to die of suicide,

four times more likely to die of injuries related to accidents, and

fourteen times more likely to die from homicide. [360]

Researchers believe the greater frequency of death from accidents and homicide may be linked to higher rates of suicidal or risk-taking behavior. In 2012, two additional studies of women in Denmark showed similar results. The first found that the risk of death remains higher for women who have had an abortion in each of the first ten years following the abortion. The second found that the risk of death increases with each abortion: 45 percent after one abortion, 114 percent after two, and 192 percent after three or more. [361, 362] An Elliot Institute review of the Finland study suggests "that induced abortion produces an unnatural physical and psychological stress on women that can result in a negative impact on their general health."[363] And, in some cases, death.

A 2011 study published in the *British Journal of Psychiatry* reviewed data from 22 published studies and found a link between abortion and mental health difficulties. The meta-analysis of studies looked at 877,181 participants, of whom 163,831 had undergone an abortion, finding, "Women who had undergone an abortion experienced an 81 percent increased risk of mental health problems."[364]

The study found increased risks of the following separate mental health effects for women who had abortions:

anxiety disorders (34 percent),

depression (37 percent),

alcohol use/abuse (110 percent),

marijuana use/abuse (220 percent), and

suicide behaviors (155 percent).[365]

In addition to the research above, postabortion-effects researcher Dr. David Reardon reports that at least 21 studies show a link between abortion and substance abuse.[366]

A 2003 study from Reardon's Elliot Institute found that women having abortions were 160 percent more likely to seek psychiatric care in the ninety days afterward than were women who had delivered their children. The study, published in the *Canadian Medical Association Journal*, reviewed the medical records of 56,741 California Medicaid patients and found that the frequency of psychiatric treatment was significantly higher for at least four years following abortion.[367]

Dr. Bryan C. Calhoun, professor and vice-chair of the Department of Obstetrics and Gynecology at West Virginia University-Charleston, says the side effects of abortion are broad ranging and inevitable:

> As certain as the effect of the law of gravity on a person who jumps from a bridge, so are the certainty of the effects that we've seen on women's health on the person who violates the moral law in taking an innocent life.

Calhoun says over the last forty years, abortion has been a health disaster for women and a public health disaster in the United States, one which costs the nation more than $1.2 billion annually.[368]

It also takes its toll on close family members.

Impact on Other Family Members

While women are greatly impacted physically and emotionally by abortion, other family members are negatively impacted, as well. In what has become known as PASS (post-abortion survivor syndrome), the siblings of aborted babies may deal with very difficult emotional struggles.

Millions of young Americans have aborted siblings. If and when the surviving children come to the knowledge that they were chosen to live while their siblings were not, they may wrestle with very difficult questions.

"The most prominent symptom of PASS is existential guilt, 'I feel I don't deserve to be alive,'" says Dr. Philip Ney, head of the Department of Psychiatry at Royal Jubilee Hospital in Canada.

"Other symptoms include pervasive anxiety, fear of the future, sense of impending doom, self-injury, obsessive thinking, poor self-identity, low self-esteem, self-destructive behavior, fear of becoming psychotic and dissociation." [369]

PASS may start at a very young age, and the child doesn't even necessarily have to be told of the previous abortion(s). "There is increasing evidence that even very young children may be aware of maternal abortions despite family attempts to maintain secrecy," according to a 1984 study. The study found that a five-year-old girl's "withdrawn regression was related to her mother's multiple abortions and her own fear of being destroyed through maternal aggression." [370]

Abortion's Impact on Men

While this book's main purpose is to properly show abortion for what it is—the exploitation of women and children at the hands of men—not all men are exploiting women. Men often experience negative and harmful effects from abortion, whether they wanted the abortion or not.

That's the verdict of the little research that has been conducted on this issue. The scarcity of scientific investigation into abortion's effects on men is probably because society regards abortion as a women's issue. It's something that, supposedly, is of no consequence to men. But the reality is exactly opposite. Miscarriage is a similar issue; according to a study published in 2010, a major myth surrounding miscarriage is that it does not affect men, citing case studies of fathers whose sadness and grieving were dismissed by others.[371] In truth, miscarriage "results in higher 'difficulty coping' and 'despair' scores on the Perinatal Grief Scale" for men than for women, according to a 2007 review of reports about abortion's impact on men.[372]

That review examined the limited studies conducted between 1973 and 2006 and found a few common themes. "At the least," researcher Dr. Catharine T. Coyle summarized, men:

> struggle with ambivalence both before and after abortion. While abortion seems to bring a sense of relief, other emotions including anxiety, grief, guilt, and powerlessness are also reported consequent to abortion.

Coyle also noted a "tendency among men to defer the abortion decision to their female partners as well as a tendency to repress their own emotions in an attempt to support their partners."[373]

In a subsequent review of the psychological effects of abortion on men, Coyle concluded: "Men may suffer intense grief after abortion as well as regret, helplessness, guilt, anxiety, anger, and emasculation." The abortion experience may be so profound as to cause post-traumatic stress disorder and lead men to self-medicate using controlled substances. The range of symptoms experienced by postabortive men, Coyle explains, may include "anxiety, persistent thoughts about the lost child, difficulty concentrating, sleep disturbances, and other somatic complaints such as headaches or palpitations."[374]

With 55 million abortions performed in America since 1973, millions of men have been party, willing or unwilling, to an abortion decision. More and more men are going public with their own pain and suffering caused by abortion. Their words are heartrending.

A married father of two who, with his wife's agreement, aborted their third child:

> Hardly a day goes by that I don't shudder and almost weep again for the murder I helped to bring about. Quite often I even wake up in the morning thinking painfully of the undeniably selfish act I did over 11 years ago—STILL! I know I overrode in my core being my conscience (dulled at the time) and my Fatherhood instinct. No two ways about it: I acted—no, I *was* a coward. My action, despite my confession and repentance before my Creator—continues to rob much of the joy from my life.[375]

A man who at seventeen convinced his girlfriend to have an abortion looks at the experience twenty-four years later:

> It's amazing to think that back then we thought our lives would be ruined with the birth of a baby. Twenty-four years later, we both know that our lives would have been significantly better if we had kept the child. Twenty-four years of pain and suffering could have been avoided if we had just dealt with a few months of disappointing friends and family. The true friends and family would have eventually come around and supported us—we know that now. We could have had our daughter, who would be graduating college by now. We would not have

gone through the depression and struggles that we did. If we only kept the baby. . . . [376]

A good friend shared his own hard and painful journey after multiple abortions in this account:

By my mid-twenties, I had been a part of three unplanned pregnancies with three different women. All three women wanted abortions, and I was more than happy to pay for all three. Back then all my thoughts were completely self-centered, and a child was not in the plans. I can remember feeling a small amount of guilt, mainly because these women had to undergo a very unpleasant procedure. And I knew, deep down, that abortion was wrong, but I quickly and easily got over it and moved on with my life.

Years later, I had gotten married and, during my second year of marriage, became a Christian. My eyes had been opened to all my sins. The three abortions weighed heavily on my heart, and I asked for forgiveness from Jesus Christ. I knew I was forgiven, and I felt His forgiveness! I remember thinking, all of my repressed guilt was gone, and I'll never have to deal with abortion again.

A year later, my beautiful daughter was born, and I was the happiest dad on earth. Then, six months later, my wife comes to me late on a Friday night and says, "I'm pregnant again, but I don't want another baby, and I have an abortion scheduled first thing Monday morning."

159

I almost passed out from the shock. I tried like crazy to talk her out of it, but there was no stopping her. I offered to take my daughter and the baby and relieve her of any responsibility. Nothing changed her mind, and she went through with it, as planned. My heart was crushed; this was pain I had never felt. Our family was broken and torn apart by this abortion; she left me, and we eventually divorced.

The only way I made it through that time was through my faith. I have only ever told two people about this experience until recently. I was able, through the power of Jesus Christ, to forgive my former wife, and hope one day she can experience His forgiveness, as well.

The pain from that abortion will always be with me. But then I have to say a prayer and give all my pain to Jesus, or it just becomes too much.[377]

Whether by action or inaction, the man who allows or approves of abortion will suffer. Indeed, he creates a void in the relationship with the mother and, possibly, other family members. Postabortion researcher Dr. Vincent Rue describes multiple ways that abortion drives a wedge between partners, leading to isolation or dysfunctional communication patterns. These effects include:

a reduction in self-disclosures by both partners, which decreases the intimacy necessary for relationship survival;

increased use of defensive communication behaviors (e.g., interpersonal hostility);

the development of partner communication appre-
hensiveness (fear translated into avoidance behaviors),
the erosion of trust, and the evolution into a closed system of interaction, as opposed to an open and dynamic
one; and

a loss of spiritual connectedness to God and to one's
partner with the advent of guilt, shame, and isolation.[378]

Pope John Paul II commented on the consequence of the absent
male in the abortion decision and the impact on family connections:
"[I]n this way the family is thus mortally wounded and profaned in its
nature as a community of love and in its vocation to be the 'sanctuary
of life.'"[379]

Abortion has no winners. Women are emotionally torn, often
experiencing years of negative and crushing symptoms. It is becoming
clearer that men are also torn, though their symptoms may exhibit in
other ways, including violence against themselves and other people, as
well as stress syndromes. Future children are more likely to be born
prematurely, and current children are more likely to experience abuse.
And the preborn baby loses her life.

We celebrate abortion as a right, but it is, in more ways than one,
killing our families.

PART 3
Men Can End It

CHAPTER 10

The Man Void

T hough I know both men and women are reading this book, the next two chapters are addressed specifically to my Y chromosome brothers, as they are the primary focus.

Women, please read on. I believe you will find the information and perspective helpful.

In this chapter, we'll look briefly at the decline of the American male and how it has impacted (or not impacted) abortion. In the next chapter, I'll outline how men must take action if we are to save our families, communities, and nation from the horror of abortion.

Men, I'm going to be very candid with you. There are too many dead humans, destroyed women, and wrecked families lying in our wake to mince words.

Men in America have failed our nation. I put myself in that same category, so my words are for all of us.

In order to properly understand the abortion epidemic in our culture today, we must have the courage to look at ourselves. Abortion exists because of us. It is promoted because of us. It is still around because of us. And the blood of 60 million babies is on our hands, as is the havoc and harm brought to women and families for over a generation.

Whether or not you are a postabortive man, you must confront the reality of abortion in America.

Where Are the Real Men?

While Planned Parenthood enjoys a $1 billion–plus budget, the sum total budget of the largest life-affirming groups in the country is around $30 million—a mere 3 percent of what Planned Parenthood receives. The monetary effort to end abortion is a small fraction of the monetary effort to continue it.

Yet Americans spend over $13 billion on porn every year.[380] Most of those dollars, guys, are coming out of our pockets. We make plenty of room in our budgets for porn, alcohol, and other self-pleasures, but we can't seem to find money, time, or resources to rescue babies and families from abortion.

We have become a self-indulgent, undisciplined, reckless, self-pleasing generation of men. We have forgotten our place in society, and we allow the termination of a human life once every twenty-five seconds because of it. We repeat Adam's behavior time and again, avoiding responsibility for our sexual behaviors, our marriages, our families, our communities, and our nation. But we can quote statistics about sports and dark beer like geniuses.

The harshest judgment and criticism in America regarding abortion should be directed at men who treat it as a "women's issue."

Abortion is not a women's issue. It is a parental issue. It is a family issue. Our consistent denial of such is the greatest blight on what is becoming a pathetic and numb gender in America. The war for pre-born babies and their families is, by and large, being fought by women. There are precious few men who have committed themselves to ending abortion. Most life-affirming women working to stop abortion in

America are largely unaided by the ones who impregnate females and use abortion as birth control to satisfy their sexual appetites.

If men *en masse* had the backbone to enter the fray and defend the weakest among us, who knows how much progress could be made toward protecting both the children and their mothers? Indeed, our neglect and ignorance of the thousands of preborn children who are killed every day in America is the severest indictment on men who claim to love God, their wives, children, and communities.

We are the worst of hypocrites.

We like the fact that abortion has become a "women's issue." By placing all of the blame and responsibility on them for making an "informed choice," we wash our hands of responsibility and continue on our selfish way.

American men today have unbridled sexual appetites. Due to our sexually saturated culture, we can now have sex with any number of women on a regular basis. The idea of a monogamous relationship has become "old fashioned" and "traditional." So those of us who feel enlightened enjoy years of sexual freedom, moving from partner to partner when we choose, all in the name of progress.

Pregnancy, however, represents some things many men don't like. First, it means we may not get as much sex. Pregnant women may not want to have sex often, especially as pregnancy progresses. After birth, a child interrupts our sexual lifestyle. A crying baby in the middle of the night, changing diapers, and the sheer emotional force of being a parent can ruin libido. The child becomes the focus, not our sexual pleasure.

Second, pregnancy means responsibility. Now our female companion may need us to stick around and pay some bills. During pregnancy, she will be talking about cribs, baby clothes, formula, and diapers. Those things cost money and can add up quickly. Spending money on babies means less money for video games, pornography, fantasy football, and beer.

Third, pregnancy means permanence. If we commit to the child, we may need to commit to the mother. That wasn't in the plan. We are fine committing to the mother as long as we get what we want, but we like to have a back-out plan if need be. A baby? A baby means we could get locked in for life. That's not in the cards.

It would be perfect if she could get an abortion. It's quick, it's easy, and we don't have to do anything except pay for it (maybe). She'll no longer be pregnant, and we can get back to a carefree, sex-centered lifestyle.

But we really don't want this on our consciences. We would rather this be a woman thing. If abortion were a female issue, we wouldn't have to deal with the pangs of guilt.

Good news. Abortion *is* a women's issue.

We don't even have to tell her we want her to get an abortion. All she has to do is ask what we think. And we now have the opportunity to utter those famous words, "It's your decision. I'll support you in whatever you decide."

Which is the same as saying, "Go ahead and abort my child. I don't care enough about you or the baby to protect either one of you."

Plus, we already know what she will decide when we leave the decision up to her. We are removing any real security we could be providing as a man and, instead, placing the entire burden of the decision and responsibility for the child on her. She will most likely have an abortion out of panic because she realizes we aren't committed to her or the child.

It's no wonder we've made abortion a women's issue. It gives us the right to exercise our lifestyle without consequence, and we get to be a proponent of women's rights at the same time.

We satisfy our self-indulgent lusts by spending billions of dollars on sexual appetites, while thirty-five hundred preborn children die daily in America.

I now believe a large majority of men have bought the lie the media has been selling for years: that we are stupid, immature, weak people who should be thankful we have a woman around to keep us from destroying ourselves.

A generation of man-degrading media has taught us the following:

Men are unable to control their impulses.

Men are incapable of leading their families or their communities.

Men are dumber than women.

Men have no right to comment upon or engage in women's issues.

The culture has successfully convinced men, in general, that we have no voice on many issues. Even if we did, we have no right to speak out.

The Absent Church

As with most challenges in America today, the social and moral ills that impact society are the same inside and outside the Church. Despite overwhelming biblical evidence that we are to affirm innocent human life and protect it, many denominations have caved into social pressure and won't defend innocent, preborn life.

Consider this statement from the United Methodist Church:

> Our belief in the sanctity of unborn human life makes us reluctant to approve abortion. But we are equally bound to respect the sacredness of the life and well-being of the mother and the unborn child. We recognize tragic conflicts of life with life that may justify abortion, and in such cases we support the legal option of abortion

under proper medical procedures by certified medical providers.[381]

The statement is both confounding and conflicting. The United Methodist Church upholds the sanctity of human life while, at the same time, inexplicably upholding abortion in cases of the "life and well-being of the mother." If it referred to those rarest of situations where the life of the mother is actually threatened because of the pregnancy, that would be worth discussing. That situation, though minuscule in number, is indeed tragic.

However, the statement also mentions "well-being," which could mean any number of things, none of which include the possibility of death. "Well-being" might refer to financial challenge, emotional distress, or the fact she'll gain weight through pregnancy. Who knows?

The statement, purposefully ambiguous, leaves room for all sorts of interpretations, thus showing that the United Methodist Church is a proabortion denomination. A number of other churches, supposedly holding to Christian doctrine, claim to be in favor of abortion.

Though the following article appeared some fifteen years ago, it holds true today. *World* magazine, in a piece called "Silence of the Shepherds," documented the silence of ministers on the issue of abortion using three methods.[382]

First, it asked twenty well-known Christian leaders to provide a full sermon they had preached on the topic of abortion. Only six of the twenty were able to do so. Just three more supplied a sermon excerpt that addressed abortion.

Second, it used the results of a study conducted by a Regent University student for her master's thesis. She surveyed 104 pastors from evangelical, charismatic, mainline, and fundamentalist churches in the South Hampton Roads area of Virginia. Seventy-six percent of pastors agreed that life begins at conception. Sixty-nine percent said the church should speak out on abortion. Just 39 percent said they had preached a full sermon on abortion. Evangelical ministers had the highest percentage of sermons preached on abortion (58 percent).

The conclusion of Regent student Molly Stone: "The average clergyman does not actively encourage his church to be involved in pro-life activity." She observed, "Even actions that clergy say are highly acceptable are typically not performed." While 70 percent of these ministers said crisis pregnancy centers were their preferred pro-life organization, the same number said they did not support a CPC.

According to *World* editor Marvin Olasky, "Only a third ever encouraged walking in a march for life or ever showed a pro-life film. Only one-sixth had endorsed pickets or prayer at abortion clinics. Rescues had been encouraged by 7 percent."

Third, *World* asked ten well-known pro-life leaders to comment on church involvement. They were unanimous that the church is AWOL on this issue. The late Dr. John Willke, who helped found the modern American pro-life movement in the late 1960s, said the silence of America's churches is "deadly" and widespread: "You see it in every denomination."

Frederica Mathewes-Green understands the silence of the church. "From the point of view of movement activists, the response of the church has ranged from weak to wimpy," she writes. "Denominations may have grand anti-abortion statements on the books, but active support for the cause, especially at the local level, seems scant."[383]

Indeed, the problem may well be both a cause and effect. Pastors and priests may be reluctant to address abortion in church because there are so many people in church who are getting abortions. Because they don't address it, people may not understand what abortion is and the harmful impacts. So they abort. Then the church is in the awkward position of potentially alienating parishioners who are postabortive. It's a vicious cycle that only ends in death and sadness.

And abortion is frequent and customary inside the church. The Guttmacher Institute reports that fully 65 percent of women who get abortions claim to be Protestant (37 percent) or Catholic (28 percent). Some 20 percent of these women who abort and claim Christianity identify themselves as "born-again," and 15 percent of women having abortions attend a religious service once or more a week.[384]

Why is the Church so ineffective when it comes to dealing with abortion? Why are abortions virtually as prevalent inside the Church as outside?

Because men are failing our churches.

Men Being Men . . . or Women

Since 85 percent of abortions are performed on unwed mothers, it is obvious that men are failing to promote and establish marriage in its proper context.

The public debate over marriage is one I don't wish to repeat here. Regardless of your view on marriage, there are two truths about marriage that are inescapable:

Marriage provides boundaries for man's sexuality.

Marriage provides the framework of security for having and raising children.

When a man and woman take the vows of marriage, they are agreeing to remain sexually committed to one another and to remain together for the sake of the couple and their children.

172

Those oaths are broken on a ridiculously regular basis. But the problem isn't the covenant and institution of marriage. The problem is the people getting married. Men have lost their way when it comes to marriage. Mark Driscoll accurately notes that American culture is filled with "boys who can shave." These are grown men who refuse to take on their God-given masculine responsibilities and instead live in a permanent state of adolescence. Rather than shouldering the weight of manhood during their twenties, they subsist in a series of dead-end jobs, live with their parents, or take up with girlfriends, enjoying the privileges of marriage without any of its obligations.

Census Bureau data sheds light on this. In 1960, the median age of first marriage for men was 22.8, climbing to 28.6 by 2012. But another measure illustrates the so-called Peter Pan syndrome much more starkly. Sociologists link the transition to adulthood with five distinct phases: finishing school, leaving home, financial self-sufficiency, marriage, and parenthood. In 1960, 65 percent of men had made it past all five mileposts by age thirty.[385] Just one-third of thirty-year-old men had done so in 2000.[386]

Without letting men off the hook, it's true that one factor in all this is feminism, which has altered traditional roles and, in some cases, led men to say no to marriage. Just 29 percent of men ages eighteen to thirty-four say a good marriage is one of the most important things in their life.[387] If men, who are becoming increasingly selfish and self-pleasing, can have their sexual appetites fed outside the boundaries of marriage, can control their finances without "investing" in the normal aspects of a committed relationship with a female, and can avoid having children for as long as possible, why get married at all?

While twentieth-century feminism has benefits, it also has draw-backs. Writing in the *Atlantic* in 2010, Hanna Rosin, author of *The End of Men*, chronicles male decline and the rise of women:

> Man has been the dominant sex since, well, the dawn of mankind. But for the first time in human history, that is changing—and with shocking speed. . . . Earlier this year, for the first time in American history, the balance of the workforce tipped toward women, who now hold a majority of the nation's jobs. The working class, which has long defined our notions of masculinity, is slowly turning into a matriarchy, with men increasingly absent from the home and women making all the decisions. Women dominate today's colleges and professional schools—for every two men who will receive a B.A. this year, three women will do the same. Of the 15 job categories projected to grow the most in the next decade in the U.S., all but two are occupied primarily by women.[388]

Where, then, are the men?

Becoming increasingly feminized, it appears.

The media has overwhelmingly promoted the idea of stronger fe-males and weaker men. S. T. Karnick writes about the pilot episode of a since-cancelled sitcom, *Big Shots*, in which a divorced man announces: "Men—we're the new women." Karnick observes,

> [T]he war against boys seems to have created three main character patterns for the adult male of our time:

sensitive guys who want to please women; weenies and dorks who want only to be left alone to drink beer and play video games with their dork buddies; and thugs who, in rebellion against their unnatural education, are perpetually concerned with proving their toughness through increasingly loutish behavior. There are, of course, examples of decent, positively masculine males in the culture, but they are becoming increasingly over-whelmed by the products of educational and cultural feminization.[389]

Quick—try to think of a TV sitcom in recent years where the father or main leading man wasn't a weak-willed moron. *Everybody Loves Raymond? King of Queens? Two and a Half Men? The Simpsons? American Dad?*

Another reader of Karnick's article conceded he was "hard-pressed to come up with a male figure on TV that possesses strong (traditional) male characteristics and who isn't some sort of bombastic oaf who is all tough and no brains. Where are the Ward Cleavers, Mike Bradys, Cliff Huxtables who used to populate TV?"[390] Even Cliff Huxtable is probably not the best example of a strong man anymore, as the actor who played him, Bill Cosby, is currently under investigation for numerous alleged sexual exploitations of women.

Feminism in its modern form has killed other positive aspects of manhood, and men have allowed it to happen. Dr. Laura Schlessinger wryly observed:

Now it is difficult to find a man who values virginity, purity, and innocence when females dress like babes.

. . . [W]ho puts any rational stock in protecting and providing when women have said they can do and be it all without a man? Men now figure they can benefit with less pressure of responsibility and use women to insure the acquisition of more goodies. Who sees any point in sacrificing for what they see are emasculating ball-busters. They think, "Open your own door, get this seat first if you can, get a job so I can relax, you said you're equal, so you pay for dinner, you said you could have/do it all . . . so do it!" Chivalry is largely dead and feminism is the murderer.[391]

Men have allowed themselves to be portrayed as oversexed, less-than-intelligent, brutish creatures who cannot get through life without a woman leading them around. And we bought the lie and live it out.

Ironically, even abortion advocates complain about the lack of male involvement. Ann-Taylor Fleming once called for greater male involvement in support of abortion rights, stating,

I dare say that many of them have impregnated women along the way, and been let off the hook in a big, big way . . . when the women went ahead and had abortions. . . . [I]t would sure be nice to hear from all those men out there whose lives have been changed, bettered and substantially eased because they were not forced into unwanted fatherhood.[392]

Does our culture even recognize what a compassionate, disciplined, strong, and steady man looks like? Do we recognize men as protectors of their nation and their families? Indeed, the freedom and prosperity we enjoy was secured through the enormous personal sacrifice of the wealth, time, and blood of millions, led by a male majority.

So why aren't men protecting their own children and the mothers of those children when it comes to abortion?

Do Men Really Accept the Sanctity of Life?

We act according to what we believe. This is true about any aspect of life. We are creatures who behave according to our worldview.

In the book *How Now Shall We Live?*, Chuck Colson outlined the three core questions that everyone consciously or unconsciously answers and uses to order his or her life:

Where did we come from, and who are we?

What has gone wrong with the world?

What can we do to fix it?

Our core beliefs about who we are, why we are here, and what is wrong with the world dictate in large part how we behave. If we, as men, have a self-centered worldview, we behave in ways that benefit ourselves. If we, as men, have a selfless worldview, we behave in ways that ultimately benefit others.

If we believe in God, we are inclined to behave (or try to behave) in ways that reflect our love and gratitude toward Him. If we don't believe in God, we are inclined to behave in ways that reflect other relative human values. These may include honorable things such as morality, ethics, or community. Or they may reflect baser things such as vengeance, power, or chaos.

Either way, how we act, where we spend our time, and how we invest our money are all reflective of our worldview. We act according to what we believe.

A primary reason men do not rise up and protect the lives and well-being of women and preborn children is we don't really believe in the sanctity of all human life.

If we did believe that every woman has infinite value and that we, as men, should partner with them and give ourselves up for them, we would not consider abortion an option. Abortion exploits women and, as demonstrated, is harmful to their emotional, spiritual, and sometimes physical well-being. Abortion degrades females and widens the gender gap. It ultimately empowers men and demeans women.

If we did believe that every woman has infinite value and that we, as men, should partner with them and give ourselves up for them, we would not be hooked on porn, having affairs, and moving from sexual partner to sexual partner. These all destroy relationships, deter commitment, and breed insecurity.

If we did believe that every conceived human being, whether planned or unplanned, has eternal value and that we, as men, have the honor and privilege of protecting and defending innocent life, we would rise up *en masse* and fight tooth and nail for preborn children. We would not only bring our own sexuality in check so we didn't cause unplanned pregnancies, but we would demand the right to protect all innocent human beings. We would decry *Roe v. Wade*—not just on the grounds that it gives complete freedom to willfully terminate preborn life. We would decry it because it prohibits us from protecting those who are dependent on us for shelter and safety.

Why then are men not truly in support of the sanctity of life? The answer lies in our discussion about the first worldview question: Where did we come from, and who are we? The desire and passion to protect preborn life is directly correlated to our answer.

Acknowledging variations, Americans generally fall into one of two camps regarding origin. We were created, or we evolved. Many major world religions claim that a Creator brought the world and humankind to life. A life form higher than ours designed us, gave us life, and put us here.

If this is our belief, we are inclined to believe that this Being had some reason or rationale for creating us. While deists hold to the belief that God created us and then left us alone to grow and develop as a planet, other religions show a God who is intimately involved and working in and through His creation.

Because this Creator is higher and wiser than us, He has a plan for us. And, as men, we concede that the Creator works through us, even when things do not go as we planned here on earth.

Thus, the answer to "Where did we come from?" for this worldview is "From the Creator." That knowledge gives value to life and purpose to existence.

If we believe we evolved, without any intervention from a higher being, the value of life is not determined by a being other than us. We value life as we see fit. That valuation may be based on numerous factors including philosophy, culture, social conditions, financial conditions, and so on.

This group of men holds to the belief that the answer to the question "Where did we come from?" is "We evolved through no intervention from any other higher being."

The second part of the worldview question and its answer stem naturally from the first part. The person who holds to a Creator of some sort naturally knows that the answer to "Who are we?" is "We are created beings, formed by a higher being." The person who believes in evolution answers the "Who are we?" query by saying, "We are evolved beings who came about by chance."

The reason this is vital to man's defense of the preborn is value. Our worldview determines how we value each other and human life in general. If we believe we are created by a higher being, our value is not self-determined. The higher being has the prerogative to assign our value. If we are evolved, the value of human life is defined by us. There is no one above us to answer to, so we can assign value to life as we see fit.

So, the reason many men in America do not actively work to defend innocent human life is because they don't believe we are created by a higher being who has a purpose and plan for life. Instead, many men believe we have evolved, giving us the authority and power to assign value to human life in whatever manner we choose.

There are many examples of male atheists who are life affirming, and I applaud them. They assign value to life on moral or ethical grounds rather than a Creator's decree. As we have seen, there are numerous fully supported arguments against abortion based on societal, legal, logical, or moral factors, and some of these rest on the value of life, whether determined by man or the Creator. The difference is, of course, that value assigned by man can change at will, whereas value assigned by a higher being is not subject to human variables.

Examples of the arbitrary assignment of value abound in world history. Modern slavery is simply the devaluation of one population by another to serve its purposes. Sex trafficking is the devaluation of certain groups of women to serve the purpose of other, typically male, groups. Abortion is the devaluation of human life, based on stage of development, to serve other humans who are farther along in that development.

All of these examples are, of course, discriminatory. Slavery discriminates based on race, sex trafficking is (generally) discrimination based on gender, and abortion involves discrimination based on both race and gender, adding stage of development as another basis for discriminating.

How does abortion discriminate in so many ways? Abortion is rooted in eugenics, which is typically grounded in racial discrimination. Abortion exploits women, so it discriminates along gender lines. And abortion discriminates against a less mature human being, in that the preborn child is not yet mature enough to speak, express herself, or sue the offending party. It also discriminates based on handicap (over two-thirds of preborn babies diagnosed with Down syndrome in America are aborted).

Ironically, American culture is now repulsed by slavery and sex trafficking. We find racial and gender discrimination distasteful and unacceptable. We have yet to fully understand the more complete discrimination against women and children entailed by abortion.

Men don't necessarily consider their internal beliefs and worldview when advocating abortion (whether actively promoting and engaging in it or passively ignoring it). However, every man that allows and acknowledges abortion as the right and moral thing to do logically and unmistakably assigns an arbitrary and reduced value to mother and child. We can then conclude a proabortion male agrees that we are not created but evolved—and thus can determine our own value.

Or these men do believe in a Creator and ignore or disagree with how value is assigned to human life. Ignorance plays a pivotal role in the cultural application of abortion. Many men who claim to have faith in

God are in favor of abortion, but they are so because they either aren't serious about that faith or they haven't studied its tenets, making their religion weak and inarticulate. Then there are men who are life affirming until an unplanned pregnancy happens in their world. A father, a boyfriend, a husband politically supports the life-affirming effort until a pregnancy becomes an inconvenience in his personal life. Conviction is lost, and he becomes a hypocrite—proud to publicly support the defense of preborn life, while privately condoning abortion.

Either way, these men were never serious or committed to the protection of innocent human life and gender equality in the first place.

Tempting Philosophies

While many men do claim to be life affirming and refuse abortion in their private lives, there are still subtle philosophies that chip away at our resolve.

The major arguments are:

Abortion is a women's issue.

Human life progresses in value as it matures.

Abortion is a just and proper means to avoid other social ills, such as overpopulation, abandonment, and financial strain on governments.

Life-affirming groups just want to save babies and ignore the negative consequences of birth on the family. They want to rescue children from abortion and just care about saving life, not caring for her after birth.

We should not be focused on abortion—we should be focused on unplanned pregnancy prevention.

1. Abortion is a women's issue.

We've dealt with this in great detail. It is only worth noting here to make one other point: many men who are life affirming genuinely believe there is nothing they can do about the abortion holocaust. Because *Roe v. Wade* took away men's right to protect their own preborn children, and because media and government continue to relentlessly repeat the false idea that abortion is confined to the female gender, these men are inclined to shy away from engaging the issue. They believe they have no power or right to fight for the preborn and true gender equality.

2. Human life progresses in value as it matures.

Because the abortion community can no longer maintain that life in the womb is a "clump of cells" or "fetal tissue," their argument has evolved. Since medical science has proven beyond reasonable doubt that human life begins at conception, and that the new life is a separate and distinct individual with two parents, abortion now becomes a question of the value of life—not the existence of life itself.

Others have covered this vital point in great detail (see Scott Klusendorf's *The Case for Life*). The progressive-valuation approach can seep into the thinking of life-affirming men, eroding a commitment to the preborn and their mothers.

The core idea of progressive valuation is that the child grows in value as she matures. Aborting before the child has reached a certain stage of development is acceptable based on various factors. These may include so-called viability, the ability to feel pain, certain organ development, sentience, etc.

Progressive valuation is a slippery slope and, to the life-affirming man, irrelevant. The life-affirming man recognizes that the preborn child has infinite value at the time she is created and that her value is dependent on what sort of being she is, not on her stage of development (or any other variable factor). In other words, a preborn child is as alive at one week as she is at forty weeks—and as dead at both stages of development if aborted.

The progressive-valuation approach attempts to make a black-and-white issue grey.

There are men who believe abortion prior to a certain stage of development is acceptable. This view is not a life-affirming view; it is an abortion-favoring view. And it is a view that allows man's subjective view of value, based on development, to dictate life and death.

3. Abortion is required to keep other social ills at bay.

At Human Coalition, I regularly receive e-mails from well-meaning people who are genuinely concerned about social welfare. I am often asked why we should save babies from abortion when we have so many born children on welfare, in the foster care system, in drug-infested homes, and so forth.

Though I understand and share the concern for children in American society, the underlying premise of the question is disturbing.

The premise is: it is better to take the lives of preborn children in order to save them from a potentially difficult life or from burdening the national social system.

More simply, it is better to kill than to let live.

The question and its premise are filled with illogical assumptions and conundrums. Here are just a few:

To assume it is better to be dead than alive is not a test-able theory. Since most of us have not died and come back to life, there is little evidence to support that death is preferable to life. While many faiths hold that the preborn and infants are ushered into a positive afterlife, these faiths do not advocate intentionally causing death in order to find out if it is true.

Ironically, we are horrified and saddened by suicide. When someone voluntarily elects death over life, assuming that death is better than life, we call it a tragedy. But when parents voluntarily take the life of their preborn child, assuming death is better than life, we call it a right and a choice.

When children grow up in difficult circumstances, it can be sad and challenging. Whether it is a foster home, a poverty-stricken home, a fatherless home, or some other real challenge, the community should be a help and assistance to the child. But should we terminate a life in order to prevent the struggle? Can we not understand that struggles and challenges are part of being human and, in an abundance of cases, contribute to our health, growth, productivity, and success as humans?

While there remain too many sad circumstances of young people from single-parent homes getting involved with drugs, alcohol, abuse, and violence, there is a multitude of examples of young people conquering those demons and rising to amazing levels of personal and professional success. President Barack Obama is just one example of a person raised in a single-parent home in less than desirable circumstances. He rose to the most powerful position in the world.

Is it really up to us to take a life before allowing her a chance to experience life in its fullness, with its joys and sorrows, triumphs and struggles, laughter and tears?

This premise is population control in disguise. It assumes that being poor, living in foster homes, or growing up in a disadvantaged community makes you less of a person. The life-affirming man sees wonderful potential, redemption, and value in each person, regardless of race, color, socioeconomic status, or government program.

We also forget that living Americans are typically highly productive. Researcher Dennis Howard calculates that we have lost around $45 trillion in gross domestic product to abortion since 1973.[393] Why is Social Security failing? One reason is that we've terminated the lives of people who were to help pay for it.

In addition, when society takes the role of determining which innocent person lives or dies, it takes a dangerous turn difficult to reverse. If society can determine the value of preborn life, it can determine the value of any other life.

4. "You just want to save babies. You do nothing to help those who are born."

I hesitate to even include this point because of its ridiculousness, but this perspective does seem to erode man's desire to protect life. It is a form of intimidation that abortion proponents use to silence others.

The idea is, if you are working to protect babies and women from abortion and not adopting, providing foster care, or mentoring someone, you are not really concerned about life. You are just concerned about babies. Your commitment to rescue the preborn is shallow, and you are ignoring the needs of those who are already born.

The argument is logically flawed on numerous levels:

A life-affirming man acknowledges that rescuing a human life from death is a primary and urgent goal. To say that goal should be subordinated to the care of a living person not in danger of death is problematic. Should we close all emergency rooms and just provide care for non-life-threatening injuries? Let's shut down fire departments and build safer houses. Let's close down police departments and, instead, work on community centers.

Do we criticize ER doctors because they aren't general practitioners? Do we disdain firemen because they aren't building the homes they are protecting? Do we condemn policemen because they aren't teachers?

Of course not. Our society understands that protecting and preserving life is the preeminent goal. Providing care for the living is essential, but it does no good if we aren't saving lives from death in the first place.

The argument assumes that life-affirming men aren't engaged in other important social work. The assumption is invalid. I know of scores of life-affirming people who are heavily involved in other work, including adoption, foster care, church programs, mentoring, youth groups, social services, welfare programs, and a host of other quality-of-life initiatives. Most life-affirming people are concerned for the preborn and for families to the extent they give generously of their time, energy, and resources to save lives and to improve lives at all stages.

In any given society, people play a variety of roles. To say a life-affirming man doesn't care about society just because he works to rescue babies does not mean he isn't playing a vital part. We would say the same about someone involved in caring for a born person. We should all be grateful for people who are working to help those around them at any stage of life, and, in fact, most of us are.

5. We shouldn't work to stop abortion. We should work to stop unplanned pregnancy.

This is a common statement, even from those professing to be life affirming. They have an innate understanding that the primary causes of abortion are rooted in sexual promiscuity, pornography, the breakdown of marriage and family, and a host of other issues.

When given this statement, I'll generally reply, "So you would advocate shutting down all cancer treatment centers in order to fund more cancer research centers?"

"Or perhaps we should shut down all ERs in favor of accident prevention educational programs?"

The flaw in the statement is to assume that the abortion epidemic is a linear problem. If we stop the cause, we'll stop the effect.

First, abortion is not a linear problem. It is more of a matrix with a host of causes, effects, symptoms, conditions, and circumstances. Secondly, refusing to stop abortions in favor of only doing prevention work results in millions of deaths and family ruin. To ignore the deaths in favor of prevention is to devalue those lives along with abortion proponents. It is akin to converting ambulances into hearses.

This is not to say we shouldn't be working hard to identify and help stop the causes of abortion. But to do so at the expense of saving children, right now, today, is horribly unethical and egregious.

Additionally, in many cases, an unplanned pregnancy *is* the catalyst for a positive change in the life of the parents. Sometimes the boyfriend will be prompted to seek gainful employment to provide for his unexpected child. A mother may finally get off drugs because she now cares for someone else more than for herself. Grandparents enter the picture and find themselves renewed with the task of helping to care for a grandchild.

We tend to think of an unplanned pregnancy as universally negative. But, as all parents know, a baby changes everything. And those changes can very often be extremely positive for the entire family, even if the baby was not expected. A baby often brings out the best in us, teaches us self-sacrifice, and can be the catalyst to tremendous growth and life change for the parents and extended family.

At this point, you might be exasperated. Men are apparently complete pigs, unable to control their sexual urges. They have been so feminized as to be almost unrecognizable. Most men ignore abortion, and many are quiet supporters of it—both inside and outside the church. Those who support and affirm life are few and far between. And they are constantly tempted to give up their passion and commitment due to strong social forces, intimidation, and the inability to legally do anything about it. The culture firmly believes men are meaningless in the abortion decision, and most men have accepted that fate.

Really, is there anything men can do to truly promote gender equality, rescue preborn children, and save the American family from the abortion holocaust?

Yes.

We can end it.

CHAPTER 11
Men Can End It

I grew up in a stable, caring home with parents who have now been married for over fifty years. I stayed away from trouble through high school and studied music in college. One night at a social event, I looked across the room and saw a beautiful woman. Jessica was captivating, and I was hooked. Six months later, I asked her on a date. A few years later, I married her.

We started life together as a couple in Pittsburgh, Pennsylvania. I started working part time at a local radio station, and my wife worked as an elementary school teacher. We were active in our church, in our community, and had all the typical hopes and dreams of young, married couples.

A few years later, Jess became pregnant. We were excited and scared, like most new parents. The pregnancy had its ups and downs, but on October 28, 1999, our first son was born. I was twenty-six years old.

My upbringing, education, and young married life couldn't have been more normal. I grew up in church, followed the teachings and leading of Jesus Christ, and tried to be a good guy. Most people liked me, and I liked most people.

I was passionately supportive of life-affirming efforts if anyone asked me. I knew the Bible verses about life, and we donated to a local pregnancy resource center. I even gave them some free consulting.

But sitting in that delivery room in October of 1999, holding my own son, my firstborn, something changed. A new life was sitting in my arms. Helpless, innocent, and . . . mine.

I remember contemplating the gravity of abortion at that moment, wondering how we, as a culture, could end so many helpless, innocent lives. My baby, my son, could have just as easily been aborted if my life had been different.

That day was the beginning of a new journey. I began to intentionally research and learn more about abortion and its impact on women, men, and society.

Eight years later, a good friend of mine asked if I wanted to do some groundbreaking work to rescue babies from abortion.

Two years after that, Human Coalition (then called Online for Life) was born. We now work to rescue families from abortion across America, using technology, data, compassion, grace, and education as our tools. Human Coalition employs quite a few men—all of whom have committed themselves to helping end abortion in America.

I tell you this story for one reason: to admit that I spent the majority of my life blissfully unaware of the harm, hurt, discrimination, and death that abortion demands. I knew abortion existed, but I did nothing—nothing—to help anyone. I was content to live in my safe, comfortable bubble, free from any responsibility to rescue babies and parents from abortion.

Over the last few years, I've had the honor of speaking with numerous postabortive men and women. Their stories have further awakened me to the pain and tragedy of abortion. And I now realize that abortion's tentacles reach far beyond the baby in the womb. They stretch out to hurt parents, siblings, extended family, communities, states, and our nation.

Abortion is not *an* issue. It is THE issue.

So, men, what now? Are you like me? Going about your life, acknowledging that around one in three adults is postabortive, that a child loses his or her life every twenty-five seconds, that abortion has wreaked havoc on virtually every aspect of American life? Did you assume abortion was just a women's issue, instead of a plague that is destroying women's rights and gender equality?

If you've read this far and remain firmly in support of abortion, I want to thank you for taking the time to read a contrary book. Few people make the effort to read books that articulate opposing views. You and I are in disagreement, but I welcome your feedback and look forward to productive dialogue in the future. I am well aware that many, many people hold fast to the idea that abortion is a woman's right, is central to women's health, and elevates women in society. I hope I've given you some facts and perspectives to think about.

Perhaps you were uncertain about abortion's impact on women and society and this book has caused you to think more often and more critically about abortion. Keep questioning, keep learning, and keep digging. There is far too much at stake to walk away and do nothing.

And if you are in the category of men who have been awakened, emboldened, and convicted by the book, I urge you to read on. If you were already pursuing true gender equality by working to end abortion in America, allow me to say thank you. Let's move forward together.

As noted earlier, women will not be restored to true equality with men, and preborn lives will not be rescued from abortion for good, until men, *en masse*, rise up to partner with women in the effort. This is not a sexist statement. It is reflective of the unified effort required to move a country from accepting abortion to being repulsed by it.

Is it possible? Of course it is. Men and women joined together in the 1800s to stem abortion in a movement that was effective for decades. Other dark times in history have been enlightened through men and women working together. William Wilberforce took a five-thousand-year tradition of slavery and turned it on its head in one lifetime, and he engaged women and men in the quest to rid the vast British Empire of that grave social injustice.

Throughout history, great movements in social justice have come about when men and women partnered together.

So, men, here are the steps to rise from silence, join our sisters and brothers who are already gaining ground, and drive abortion from America's shores.

All Men

Get off the damn porn. Stop sleeping with someone other than your wife. Stop moving from woman to woman, using them for your own selfish gratification and then tossing them away when you are done with them.

It's sleazy, disrespectful, self-centered, and you give our gender a bad reputation.

Plus, you are going to get someone killed. Like an innocent baby. Or two.

Porn

There is precious little research on the connection between pornography and abortion, mainly because there are very few research organizations willing to take on the topic. Plus, the vast majority of money is poured into abortion-favoring research groups.

Porn is a huge, extremely powerful industry.

So, while there is very little credible work being done on this connection, allow me to posit a theory.

Porn has been linked to sexual promiscuity for decades. It has been identified as a cause of extramarital affairs and multiple sex partners. A Marriage and Religion Research Institute report concludes, "[U]sers of pornography have a higher likelihood of contracting a sexually transmitted disease or fathering an out-of-wedlock pregnancy."[394]

It's obvious that promiscuity of any sort opens the door to a host of STIs, including HIV and AIDS. There are 20 million new STIs each year, and a total of 110 million infections among men and women in the United States, according to the Centers for Disease Control. The cost to treat these infections is $16 billion annually.[395] And it's completely avoidable. For the unmarried, abstinence is the only form of truly "safe sex" known to man (or woman), and for married couples, faithfulness inside marriage will allay any and all concerns. "You have an extremely minimal chance of catching one of over 25 different sexually transmitted infections, many of which are incurable and can cause cancer," when you practice abstinence, as the Medical Institute for Sexual Health points out.[396]

And, I submit, sexual promiscuity also leads to unplanned pregnancies that are ending in abortion. It's not exactly rocket science to connect the dots here.

Your porn habit may result in the death of another human being. Is your porn that important to you?

Outside of the impending destruction of your marriage, other relationships, and your own character, there is the potential death of a preborn child.

Look, every red-blooded American man is tempted by porn, including yours truly. We are surrounded by it, saturated by it, and we can't get through an NFL game without being confronted with it.

And there are many guys who are full-on addicted to it. For them, it's not a habit—it's a necessity.

Gentlemen, there is nothing good that comes out of porn. Nothing. Do not pass "Go;" do not collect $200. Get all of the help, accountability, counseling, and intervention you need. You may end someone's life if you don't.

Stop Having an Affair

I have had the privilege of counseling men who have had affairs. Every one of them would tell you it was a horrible, costly mistake. They would openly confess they traded cheap sex for a lasting, committed relationship. All it brought was pain.

Similar comments are shared anonymously on the Internet[397] by other men who have had affairs:

> "Even if you're in a bad place in your marriage, the deceit will weigh on you and it's just not worth it in the end. My exploits will probably send me to the grave a decade earlier than scheduled. And for what? Some cheap thrills. . . ."
>
> —Attorney, thirty-two

> "Having an affair was the stupidest mistake I've ever made. . . . My wife freaks out if I don't check in at least once an hour when I'm doing anything without her. I feel like I'm being watched *all* the time. Even now."
>
> —Struggling actor, twenty-seven

"[E]verything came to a crashing halt when I gave my wife chlamydia, which I'd contracted from my side dish. As far as STDs go, chlamydia isn't so bad. But in terms of all the possible ways a guy can get caught, infecting your wife with a disease—even a relatively benign, curable one—isn't something I'd recommend."

—Photojournalist, thirty-three

"I feel awful about betraying my life partner. I was sleeping with a colleague for two years before my wife accidentally picked up my phone and saw an incriminating text message thread, and things haven't been the same since. We're trying to work everything out through counseling but my wife is understandably angry. I don't know if her rage will ever subside. A scorned woman never forgets, right?"

—Customer service representative, twenty-eight

Guys, an affair is also an abortion risk, plain and simple. You cheat on your wife: you get the other woman pregnant. Now your secret has turned into living, breathing evidence of your indiscretion. The logical solution? Abort the child, and no one is ever the wiser.

Go work on your marriage. We tend to think all of the stuff that is wrong in our marriage is her fault. News flash: it is most likely our fault. Fix yourself, and your marriage will improve. You are probably the problem, anyhow.

Stop Sleeping Around

You unmarried guys who like to bed multiple women are a huge risk to preborn children—and an affront to the female gender. And you make the rest of us look bad. Not only are you unwilling to commit to a woman before you sleep with her, you don't have the decency to commit to her when you get her pregnant.

I know we live in a sex-saturated culture. I know we continue to treat traditional marriage like it is old fashioned and out of style. I know abstinence is treated like pure folly in the public schools and many other venues.

You are the men who love the power that abortion affords you. You are the men who drive the abortion industry, line the pockets of abortion providers, and are famous for saying, "It's your decision, honey. I'll support you in whatever you decide."

As much as I'd love to say kind and sensitive things to you, here's the truth. You are a petulant little boy who never grew up. You use women to satisfy the sexual urges you don't have the discipline and maturity to control. You talk about women's rights and equality because it gives you a pass on your lifestyle, and you are the first in line to defend abortion rights. And you only do that so that you can continue to sleep with whomever you want.

Grow up. Find a man who has been committed to his wife for twenty years, and be like that guy. Stop modeling yourself after the mindless pimps on TV and YouTube, and acknowledge you don't give a rip about women unless they give you what you want.

You are the face of abortion and the reason women in America continue to be exploited.

A Note to Women

Would you please stop entertaining and sleeping with these guys? If you are sleeping with a married guy, you are being used. If you are sleeping with a guy who hasn't married you, you are being used. "Living together" is just a fancy term for "I want to use you for sex until I'm tired of you."

Please, kick him to the curb and go find a decent man who accepts you, treats you like an equal, and will give up his life for you. Anyone else is just a waste of time.

Besides, there is a good chance this loser is going to get you pregnant. Who is going to be left with the decision about what to do with the baby? You. Who is the only legally responsible party? You. Who will bear the brunt of the abortion? You.

You are worth more than that. You deserve to be treated better, respected more, and protected by someone who is willing to commit the rest of his life to you. Don't settle for anything less.

A Message to Postabortive Men

Allow me to address those postabortive men reading the book right now. Much of the power to end abortion rests with you. Your stories, your pain, and your perspective are what is missing from the abortion dialogue in America.

When was the last time we saw a news story about a postabortive man? It's very rare.

Aerosmith's Steven Tyler has unveiled his pain at allowing his child to be aborted. Tyler was twenty-five in 1975, when he and his fourteen-year-old live-in girlfriend decided to abort their child. "It was a big crisis," he recalled in *Walk This Way*, Aerosmith's tell-all memoir. "It's a major thing when you're growing something with a woman, but they convinced us that it would never work out and would ruin our lives."

Tyler's girlfriend, whom he later dropped, had a saline abortion, a heinous procedure in which a salt solution is used to slowly burn and kill the baby. Tyler witnessed it all. "You go to the doctor and they put the needle in her belly and they squeeze the stuff in and you watch. And it comes out dead. I was pretty devastated. In my mind, I'm going, 'Jesus, what have I done?'"[398]

After Michael Jackson's death, it was revealed he had written a song about an abortion loss, possibly his own. Recorded in the 1980s, "Song Groove (A/K/A Abortion Papers)" includes the narrator's protest of his partner's decision to abort their child:

> Those abortion papers
>
> Signed in your name against the words of God
>
> Those abortion papers
>
> Think about life, I'd like to have my child[399]

1. Start with your own heart, your own life.

These are powerful testimonies, and there are tens of thousands, perhaps millions of men who have the same story. Their stories need to be told, even if it is just to one person, one couple, one teenage kid who doesn't know the first thing about it.

Your story, though painful, is also redemptive.

If you have not yet come to grips with your own postabortive past, healing must occur first.

Charlie is a man in his seventies. He took his girlfriend to get an abortion in 1972. Shortly afterward, he straightened out his life and got married to another woman, to whom he has been wed for almost forty years. They have children and grandchildren. Still, he was never able to escape the pain and guilt he felt from that abortion, which he even kept a secret from his wife. He ultimately found healing after he attended a Rachel's Vineyard retreat for postabortive men and women.

After the retreat, he wanted to jump into some kind of life-affirming activity. So when his church encouraged his participation in 40 Days for Life, a forty-day period of prayer and fasting to end abortion, he got involved.

> He eagerly went straight to the front lines [outside an abortion facility] to pray and talk with the younger men taking women in to have abortions, sharing with them the mistake he still regretted nearly forty years later. He smiled broadly. "And now, standing here praying and sharing my story with these younger men, God is healing me. I have never felt such peace—and such joy."[400]

How can you escape the bonds of your part in abortion?

Recognize your role, take responsibility, and find healing. You may very well not have known that you were actively or passively ending a life. The mother of your child may have insisted on getting the abortion. You may have been getting pressure from family members, friends, or other authority figures to abort.

Still, you were involved and need to own up to it.

Recognizing and taking responsibility for your active or passive role in an abortion is imperative if you want to join the effort to save others.

Forgiveness, peace, and joy are all on the table for you. But taking ownership and confessing your role are necessary steps.

This is not a book about postabortive counseling, but I have listed some excellent resources at the end of the book if this is a need in your life. I encourage you to immediately move toward the path to healing and recovery. Your family and relationships may depend on it. And, when you experience forgiveness and peace, you may be ready to help others avoid your struggles.

As a follower of Christ, I am absolutely certain you can find forgiveness and redemption in Him. I encourage you to seek Him out.

2. Share your story with trusted loved ones.

I'm asking you to do something that is extremely difficult. In some cases, my request may not be appropriate.

However, you may be realizing that the time has come to end your silence. There may be a family member contemplating abortion who doesn't know you were responsible for one. You may have a teenage son or daughter who believes abortion is a reasonable solution, and they have no idea the pain and tragedy you have suffered.

Your own relationships may be suffering, and you haven't been able to identify why until now. There may be strain, distance, and anger for reasons that are now known.

I don't make this request lightly, and I urge you to carefully consider the cost of sharing your story. You might consider seeking the counsel of a trusted friend, a priest, a pastor, or a counselor before you tell a family member. You could very well risk harming relationships, being ashamed, and creating tension between you and others if you share your past.

Your story could also mean the difference between life and death for a preborn child. And your story will very likely save the life of a child not yet conceived. Your story may be enough to convince a family member who currently sees abortion as a solution that it is, in fact, terribly damaging to all involved. Your life-ending decision years ago could save a life in the future.

3. Speak your testimony publicly.

Share your story with a broader audience.

This takes a lot of guts, guys. There isn't a man alive who, having come to grips with his abortive past, wants to tell strangers about it. And this isn't an appropriate step for all men.

But it is for many of you. And we won't end abortion in America until those of you who can, do.

Why? Because those forces and organizations who actively promote abortion fear you most. Your courage to take responsibility for the abortion, to admit you used and exploited a woman, and to admit your mistakes is the most powerful tool in the effort to end abortion.

The reason is this: it takes a strong man to admit he has wronged someone. It takes a strong man to share that publicly. We need strong men.

And your story is not only about failure and harm; it is about redemption and moving forward. It is about using your mistakes and selfishness and turning them into triumphs and selflessness.

When America learns that thousands, tens of thousands, even hundreds of thousands of men are willing to admit their abortions were wrong, that they harmed women, children, and families, America will begin to wake up and realize we've made an awful, horrendous mistake.

And we will work together to rectify that mistake.

You may be shamed; you may be judged. You may lose friends or family members. I certainly hope that isn't the case. But I promise you that you'll also have advocates, supporters, and companions. And you can count me among them.

There is a safe, nonpolitical, nonpartisan site for men and women who wish to share their postabortion stories. Whether or not you choose to remain anonymous, I invite you to share your story at www.AbortionMemorial.com. This site is intended to be an appropriate, honoring place for postabortive parents who want to heal.

All Men Who Want to End Abortion

Consider Brendon's story:

"Brendon, will you sit down?" my seventeen-year-old girlfriend said. "I need to tell you something."

It had been less than twenty-four hours since I had joyfully thrown my red graduation cap into the air at my high-school graduation. I was an eighteen-year-old, beach-obsessed California "bro" headed to Southern Methodist University in Dallas, Texas. I was on top of the world. I could be anyone I wanted to be and do anything I wanted to do when I got to college.

"As you know," she continued, "I've been feeling sick over the past couple of weeks, and . . ." She trailed off.

We had decided that we weren't going to date in college, so I assumed this picnic at the park Emily had prepared was a nice gesture to celebrate graduation. We had dated on and off, a very typical high-school relationship: I was immature, and it led to less-than-solid choices. I knew they were wrong deep down, but everyone was doing them, so it was normal.

"Brendon . . . I'm pregnant," she blurted out. I scrambled to my feet in time to throw up in the bushes.

Thoughts raced through my head. Emily explained that her parents knew, they had discussed it, and that the baby would be born. We'd figure out whether we'd keep the baby or whether she'd be adopted.

After that fateful picnic, my initial reaction was, *I know an easy way out of this . . .* Thank God we had people to steer us away from abortion and introduce us to options.

Little did I know that God had an amazing plan to redeem our sin. By no means was the pregnancy pretty. I was at SMU while Emily was at a community college, pregnant, in San Diego. I can't imagine how uncomfortable life was for her at that time. On top of all that, finding adoptive parents who were a good match was surprisingly more difficult than we imagined. There were a number of very tough phone calls, and keeping the baby was becoming more and more likely.

Late in the pregnancy, God used Sarah Jensen-Elhoff at the Adoption Center of San Diego to match our baby to the most amazing parents. Tommy and Karen had recently moved to California from Texas to be close to Karen's ailing mother. They had battled through fertility treatments and years of disappointment, finally deciding that having biological children would be unlikely.

Open adoption was a new concept to me. Instead of placing your child with a family and never seeing the baby again, in an open adoption you have the opportunity (not the requirement) to develop a relationship with the adopted baby and his or her adoptive family. *That's a good idea*, I thought. *When the baby gets to an age where she is curious who her biological parents are and why we placed her for adoption, she can ask us.* I completely underestimated what form this was actually going to take.

Abby was born in January of 2007. She is the most amazing nine-year-old I have ever met. Everyone first comments on how beautiful she is, and how right they are: she is beautiful. But if you get the pleasure of spending five minutes with her you see that her heart is exponentially more radiant. She is so incredibly loving and kind. She's witty, intelligent, and humorous beyond her age. Her laugh lights up a room.

And I, the same guy who considered an abortion an option, have the opportunity to know her and spend substantial time with her. Since her birth, her parents have welcomed me as a little brother of their own. I am now married to my beautiful wife, Kate, and they have welcomed her with open arms as well. Abby calls her "Miss Kate." We see them often, vacation together, and celebrate holidays together. They are family.

Scripture says that "in love he [God] predestined us to adoption as sons through Jesus Christ to Himself, according to the kind intention of his will" (Ephesians 1:4–5). People ask me all the time what Abby calls me. I understand why people ask, but it strikes me as a funny question every time. Abby is not my daughter; I am not her father. Just as God has chosen us as sons and daughters because it was pleasing to him, Abby has been chosen and grafted into her family. She is Tommy and Karen's daughter, and they are her father and mother. I am just eternally grateful that God takes painful and inconvenient, albeit self-inflicted, circumstances and makes them more beautiful than I could have ever imagined.[401]

Brendon's story is about a man who admittedly made some mistakes. But he owned them. He took responsibility for them, and he made things right. And, in the end, his mistakes turned into unspeakable blessing. Brendon's story could have ended differently—an aborted child, ruined relationships, and family destruction. Instead there was new life, a marvelous gift for a wonderful couple, and redemption and restoration. Brendon made a choice, and that choice made all the difference in the world.

We won't end abortion in America until men individually choose to live their lives in a manner that rejects selfishness. Abortion exists because of male selfishness. And it will continue to exist as long as men continue to seek their own power, control, and pleasure.

Let's review the two primary social reasons abortion was promoted by men: population control and eugenics.

Population control is, as evidenced by its name, about control. It's about power. It's about one group having the authority to control another. One group decides a population needs to be curbed or eliminated altogether because they believe they are smarter and more advanced than the other group.

The rationale may be trumped up with well-intended sentiments. The group in control may be trying to ensure that the world has enough food, that poverty is eliminated, or that education thrives. All of those are worthwhile endeavors.

But all of those may be addressed without aborting humans or sterilizing women.

The issue of starving people in the world is not about the abundance of food. The world produces more than enough food for every person on the planet.[402] Poverty is a drastic and real problem in many nations. But is the primary issue the size of the population or other pivotal factors such as corruption, economic climate, social discrimination, or form of government?

The same logic applies to the uneducated and illiterate. Is it the size and reproductive rate of the populace that is to blame for the state of education, or are the primary causes related to culture, form of government, and the disposition of people in power?

There is a vast difference between educating a family and forcing a populace to practice population control. There is a vast difference between an individual family choosing to use non-abortive means to determine the size of their family and a group in power dictating the size of their family.

The first is an attempt to empower; the second is an attempt to overpower.

Eugenics has the guts to admit it is population control for only certain races or people groups. It takes the position that one race should have the right to determine the growth of another.

This is also disguised in socially acceptable language. Eugenics promotes the control over another race for its own good. They may be poor, uneducated, and unruly. So the solution is to sterilize them, force them to use birth control, or make abortion a vital part of the culture, so they eliminate themselves.

There are awful assumptions embedded in these two philosophies. The primary one is that adding new members of the population increases the problems of that population. Yet, often population growth can actually help solve the problems ailing a nation and help it flourish. Would anyone doubt that America has grown more technologically and medically advanced—and stronger as a nation—as its population has increased?

This doesn't mean growth doesn't have challenges. But America is the wealthiest, most prosperous nation on the planet. Should we have purposefully stayed at 50 million people to limit the growth? Should an outside nation or group have a say over our own reproductive rights?

Both population control and eugenics are elitist philosophies. And they are both primarily about power—attempting to solve real needs of other people groups by addressing population growth and ignoring other primary factors that cause social challenges.

Population control and eugenics are large-scale manifestations of man's arrogance and selfishness.

The personal reason for men pushing abortion is sexual liberation. Men in America enjoy complete freedom to sleep with whomever they choose without legal, social, or cultural responsibility for the outcome of their actions related to a pregnancy.

It is the height of selfishness. Men feel they have the right to express the deepest of intimacies with women with no sign of commitment or support for said women. And our culture has devolved to the point where many women think this is just how it is.

And, when a woman has an unplanned pregnancy, the man can walk away from the situation without any responsibility.

Unplanned pregnancy is obviously an enormous factor contributing to abortions. Unplanned pregnancies are most often caused by selfish men. The solution? Stop being selfish, and then watch unplanned pregnancies decline and abortion go away.

Whether or not men are motivated by social and global reasons (population control and eugenics) or personal reasons (sexual freedom), abortion is about men exercising power and control over women, either nationally or personally.

Consequently, men must take up the mantle of service, sacrifice, and selflessness if we are to achieve true gender equality and rescue preborn children from death in the womb.

We end abortion by being respectful, moral men who see women as true equals of infinite value.

We end abortion by confronting social challenges through means other than dictating reproduction rights.

We end abortion by making a personal, committed decision to stop using women for our own sexual pleasure.

Men Ending Abortion on a National Scale

On a larger scale, there are a number of ways men can rise up and work to end abortion in America.

1. Mentor other men.

Researcher Catherine Coyle in her study, "Men and Abortion: Finding Healing, Restoring Hope," says:

> Mature male mentors are needed to teach younger men about the importance of chastity, commitment in relationships, and responsible parenting. Mentors can serve as role models as they demonstrate the behaviors that foster spiritual and psychological health in marital, paternal and fraternal relationships.[403]

Your willingness to teach, train, and share your life with other men is an essential piece of the abortion puzzle. This may or may not involve a commitment to an organization like Big Brothers/Big Sisters, a local youth group, a community organization, or a social service agency. Just working with your own sons, the neighborhood kids, or young men in your church can be a huge influence.

The editor of this edition of the book, Dr. Tim Boswell, actually shared this story with me while working on this updated version:

> It's been my privilege to be mentored by a man I respect and admire, and I would recommend this approach to anyone. His name is Guy Church, and he is about a decade my senior and about ten years farther along life's path with his marriage, career, and kids (all sons, like

210

me). Before I asked if he would mentor me, I learned the type of man he was by watching him; I got to know him building houses together in Mexico on short-term mission trips. He is a man of unflinching integrity and dedication to excellence, wholly committed to giving to and serving others. The kind of person I aspire to be. I was nervous about approaching him to start a mentoring relationship, but his willingness—and what has followed—have been the easiest thing in the world.

Perhaps "easiest" isn't the right word; sometimes it's quite difficult to open up and share about my deepest fears, worries, or frustrations, even when I know they'll be met with compassion rather than judgment. We have talked about everything from marriage to parenting, spiritual matters to life mission, midlife burnout to leaving a legacy. He knows my goals and what I'm currently working on, and he checks in and holds me accountable. For my part, I share my perspective and advice for things he's dealing with, and I hope that it's been valuable both ways. And it's not always heavy lifting—sometimes we simply chat about our families and life. Or he'll share financial counsel. Or action steps for a particular goal. Or directions to the barbecue joint with the tastiest sauce.

We meet up once a month at a coffee shop or restaurant, and although we call it "mentoring" (for that's what it is, though not a lot of guys have much familiarity with the word), there is nothing unusual about it, no high standard of admission prohibiting most from participating. This is not something only for perfect saints on one side of the table and struggling failures on the other—far from it. It's iron sharpening iron. It's the willingness of one man to pour into another, and for that man to humbly recognize that he can benefit from the wisdom and experience of the first. And then, someday, to pass it on.

This isn't rocket science, so don't be intimidated by it. If you're not sure how to begin, find someone to work through a book with you—simply read a chapter or two a month and then meet to talk about it over a cup of coffee. Use a text that gets to the heart of real issues, then speak honestly and hold each other accountable if you decide to make changes. A writer whose books speak to me is John Eldredge, author of *Wild at Heart*, but seek out resources that resonate with you.

Find a mentor, be one, or both. You won't regret it.[404]

Whether formal or informal, be a truthful role model to other men in your community. Talk about abortion, sex, marriage, pornography, and how to properly treat a woman. Keep in mind that many people are more influenced by what is caught than what is taught. In other words, live out what you say.

2. Carefully research the use of birth control.

The purpose of this book is not to discuss the moral implications of using birth control within a family. However, if you have made the decision to use birth control as a means of dictating the size of your family, do your homework.

Life begins at conception, not at implantation. If you are using a method of birth control that negatively impacts implantation, you could unknowingly be using an abortifacient substance.

Keep in mind some birth-control products state that life begins at implantation, not conception. While many in the medical community, and some pharmaceutical companies, claim that these drugs do not cause abortions, they may not properly understand the facts of life.

For more information on this very important topic, I refer you to a short brochure by Randy Alcorn called, "Does the Birth Control Pill Cause Abortions?" It is free and widely available online.

3. Become involved and help grow life-affirming organizations in your area.

When Planned Parenthood opened a surgical abortion clinic in his hometown of College Station, Texas, David Bereit reluctantly got involved, at his wife's prodding, to oppose it. He agreed to serve on the board of the Coalition for Life, the group launched in opposition to the new Planned Parenthood facility, and wound up the chairman after his first meeting. The chairman had resigned just before the meeting and, as David put it, he "didn't say 'No' fast enough." Despite his own sense of inadequacy, he saw the need and felt called to serve:

> I had no grand vision, no compelling drive to lead this
> mission. But I couldn't shake the inner conviction that
> had begun on that sidewalk. In my mind's eye I kept
> seeing the faces of the women I'd seen entering the
> abortion facility and their downcast eyes as they left.

> Everything about the place felt so wrong, and I had an inner sense that God wanted me to try to right that wrong.[405]

His initial efforts at the Coalition didn't prove fruitful, so he decided to resign his post at the end of his three-year term. But at the fundraising banquet at which his resignation was announced, the speaker, life-affirming leader Joe Scheidler, encouraged the audience to overcome their fears and do what is right even if they had no desire to do so. "There's somebody in this room who is supposed to do this work full time," Scheidler said, "somebody who is supposed to take a leadership role in this work." That caught David's attention, and he left the gathering, he writes, "with a new stirring in my heart. Maybe I did have a role."

Soon after, he and his wife came to the conclusion that he would begin seeking to end abortion full time in College Station, Texas.

> I went home and talked to Margaret. We talked to our pastor. We prayed fervently. As much as we knew we were giving up—the company car, the salary, the health benefits, all the bonuses, and fancy dinners out with the doctors—all we had to do was weigh that against the innocent children's lives and mothers' well-being at stake, and even though we were terrified, we knew this was God's call.[406]

Now Bereit helps lead 40 Days for Life, the largest life-affirming mobilization in history, an effort that has helped save more than seven thousand preborn children from abortion since 2007. To date, more than a half-million people have participated in 40 Days for

Life campaigns in 501 cities and nineteen countries. Twenty-nine abortion facilities have closed, and seventy-nine abortion clinic workers have quit as a result of 40 Days for Life campaigns.

There are a host of life-affirming organizations across the country. Some are involved politically, some judicially. Some are involved with the public, providing compassion, truth, care, and connections to other local services.

Most of these are called pregnancy resource centers, crisis pregnancy centers, or pregnancy care centers. They are typically local nonprofits who work with the abortion-minded people in their areas.

The vast majority of these centers are staffed by women; they are desperate for men as volunteers and staff. Oftentimes they have abortion-minded men coming in, and they have no mentors to talk to them.

Want to save lives and help end abortion? Get to know your local pregnancy center, and get involved.

A list of great organizations working to save women, men, and babies from abortion is included in the Resources section at the back of this book, and I encourage you to get involved. You will be glad you did. Just consider the example of one of my closest friends, my coworker Jeff Bradford; you were introduced to him in the first chapter of this book, but here is the rest of his story:

The last thing I thought I would do was work for a pro-life non-profit. For seventeen years, I owned my own company, and as the CEO I worked fifty- and sixty-hour weeks. When I was not working, my wife and I were helping start a small church in a suburb of Dallas. I was a board member and lay pastor of the church, and my wife was the worship leader. Anyone that has helped start a church knows the time demands and work required, but we were happy to be a part of it.

However, after eight years, the church split; it's a long story, but one of the "pastors" ended up in jail. The church split started my journey in dealing with an abortion that took place over twenty-four years ago. Even though my wife and I had spent years leading home teams, mentoring other men, women, and couples, we never talked about the abortion, and the pastor never spoke on the sacredness of life. After the split, my wife and I realized we had ministered to everyone else and neglected our own marriage. We needed help, so we decided to visit a Christian counselor. I will never forget how my wife began to cry uncontrollably as we entered the counseling office. I thought, *What is going on? Is our marriage in worse shape than I thought?*

As the counselor dug into the underlying issues behind her tears, we realized it came down to a decision we'd made twenty-four years ago. We were engaged to be married, and five months before the wedding, we got pregnant. Within a week of finding out, we ended up at Planned Parenthood and killed our first child through an elected abortion. That may sound harsh, but the life of our daughter was taken. And there is no one to blame but myself. My wife would never have made that decision had I not persuaded her to do so and taken her to Planned Parenthood.

This is a decision you can't take back. It's also one that sticks with you the rest of your life. Our society says, "It's OK, it's not a child." That is simply untrue. It *was* a child, *our* child, and we threw her away for the sake of convenience and to avoid embarrassing our family or ourselves. Shameful.

Can you imagine the weight I carry by admitting that we would have a twenty-four-year-old daughter living were it not for my decision to go to the abortion clinic?

Seventeen years later, God had dropped the scales from my eyes, and I saw what abortion really is. I witnessed firsthand the devastation it causes women (and men) when we come to grips with our abortions. I realized that I had done everything opposite of God's way. As a Christian man now, I recognized the wreckage I had caused by my sin. Abortion not only was the killing of my little girl but had quietly torn up my wife and had almost ripped us apart. There was a bitter root that had grown in her . . . feelings of abandonment, questioning her self-worth and whether she was of value, and beating herself up for allowing the abortion and not speaking up to rescue her baby girl. I realized that I did not fight for my wife or my daughter. Both had been abandoned by me at the time when they needed me the most. I was a twenty-one-year-old, ignorant coward who did not have the character nor the values to choose my wife or my little girl when my wife needed me to be a man and my daughter needed her daddy.

The Bible says God uses our testimony, and although we are but filthy rags, God redeems all things and turns ashes into beauty. It was not until an extremely difficult trial in our lives that God, in His generous mercy and grace, allowed us to be healed. There were lots of fights and tears, but also healing. And through it all, God in His providence started us on a wonderful journey to share our testimony and story with others in a way that would bring tremendous healing and redemption for us and for many people around the country.

The same week that my wife and I found ourselves in counseling, Brian Fisher handed me his business card for Online for Life (now Human Coalition). I knew immediately this was no coincidence. Brian mentioned that he ran an all-volunteer nonprofit, using the Internet, technology, and business principles to save babies from abortion. I about hit the floor. I remember I pulled out Brian's card that night and just shook my head, saying to God, "What are you doing?" I knew He was about to do something, and yet I did not want anything to do with it.

Well, today I work at Human Coalition, helping to raise the financial resources to end abortion city-by-city in our lifetime. It is the most rewarding work I have ever done. When you can combine business, technology, data, science, compassion, and grace to save a life and then replicate that over and over . . . it does not get any more rewarding than that.

When we are willing to share our testimony and allow God to heal us, it is amazing what He can do. Today, my wife and I have four beautiful children: two boys and two girls, the oldest nineteen years old and the youngest eleven. We have been blessed. We miss our little Sarah every day, but we know she is with the Lord and we will see her again. And we are encouraged that men and women are rising up to end this holocaust. I believe God is calling men, more than ever, to rise up and help end abortion once and for all. The Bible commands us to do so, and history proves that when the church decides to get out of her comfort zone and join God in His work, then holocausts are ended, nations are healed, and God is glorified. I pray you will join us. Bring your time, talents, and treasure, and together we will rescue every little boy, girl, mom, and dad from the devastation of abortion.[407]

4. Use your specific gifts and talents.

Laws follow culture. *Roe v. Wade* was handed down in 1973 because some very determined Americans wanted abortion to be legal. Abortion will stay legal until enough life-affirming women and men act and the culture no longer wants it so.

We are now many decades into the abortion culture in America, and our society continues to approach abortion from opposing views.

Women will continue to be harmed and used, men will continue to suffer, and babies will continue to be lost until the social tide turns against abortion.

How do we regain a society that respects women and life?

We need look no further than social reformer William Wilberforce to find the answer.

Wilberforce was a man of wealth, intellect, and position, yet he used his gifts and connections as opportunities for others' benefit. Early in his career as a member of Parliament in eighteenth-century England, he chose to vote and campaign according to his conscience rather than adhering to a political party. As Eric Metaxas writes in his biography *Amazing Grace*, "Wilberforce was one of the brightest, wittiest, best connected, and generally talented men of his day, someone who might well have become prime minister of Great Britain if he had, in the words of one historian, 'preferred party to mankind.'"[408]

His approach to ending slavery in England (and the West Indies) was remarkably comprehensive, taking advantage of most of the media of his day, various realms of influence, and numerous approaches to educating the public.

Political: Wilberforce used his power and influence in Parliament to keep the slavery issue in front of his fellow politicians for years. He continually submitted legislation to end the slave trade, though in the early years there was no chance of its passage—slavery was simply too ingrained as a part of culture, its existence too broadly accepted. In Wilberforce's day, slavery "was as accepted as birth and marriage and death, was so woven into the tapestry of human history that you could barely see its threads, much less pull them out."[409]

Not only was slavery accepted, but the trade was seen as a great benefit to England, which it was, financially; the system that took British-made goods to Africa to buy slaves, shipped those slaves to the West Indies, and transported the resulting slave-grown products back to England represented about 80 percent of the nation's foreign income.[410] Political resistance to any measures that threatened this trade was staunch, to say the least.

Wilberforce could have found plenty of excuses why fighting it was a fool's errand, or he could have claimed that his chronically poor health prevented him from championing this cause. Yet rather than being deterred, Wilberforce was relentless in repeating his message. He took his natural gifts and abilities and aimed them squarely at the heart of the opposing viewpoint, which argued that slavery was needed and good. As a parliamentary debater, even in his early years Wilberforce could often be seen "laying waste to his opponents through his sarcastic wit and extremely agile repartee," displaying "vigor and brilliance. There was a giddy abandon and fury to his oratorical sorties that no one would ever forget."[411] Wilberforce would later show great respect and deference to his political peers and opponents during the many years he sought to sway their minds, yet he kept his fire and passion. Although short, slight, and sickly, Wilberforce could command the attention of every person in earshot. Diarist and author James Boswell witnessed him speak in the House of Commons and wrote, "I saw what seemed a mere shrimp mount upon the table; but as I listened, he grew, and grew, until the shrimp became a whale."[412]

For nearly twenty years, Wilberforce brought forward bill after bill in Parliament, pleading and reasoning and trying to persuade even the most reluctant of listeners. And, near the end of his life, his hard work paid off.

Media: Wilberforce knew that he was up against something far more pervasive, and far more insidious, than even the slave trade. He was fighting against the mental outlook that accepted it as morally permissible to treat another human being as one's property. Metaxas writes:

[Wilberforce] vanquished the very mind-set that made slavery acceptable and allowed it to survive and thrive for millennia. He destroyed an entire way of seeing the world. . . . Even though slavery continues to exist here and there, the idea that it is good is dead. The idea that it is inextricably intertwined with human civilization, and part of the way things are supposed to be, and economically necessary and morally defensible, is gone.[413]

To do this, Wilberforce knew that he had to effect not just a Parliamentary vote but a cultural about-face. The British people had to not only change their minds but change their entire way of thinking, of valuing humanity and their own responsibility to protect it. To accomplish this cultural paradigm shift, Wilberforce printed bulletins, held live events (including bringing people on board slave ships to smell the stench of death and see the bloodstains), gave speeches, wrote letters, and used every educational tool available. And, with persistence, it worked. By the time slavery was made illegal in England, the culture found it repulsive. His committed and comprehensive approach to educating his nation worked.

Community Organization: Wilberforce started a very large number of associations and movements during his lifetime. Not all were specific to slavery, but all were dedicated to the betterment of society in general. Some were dedicated to the ethical treatment of animals, many were centered on promoting common decency, and others were specific to the slave trade.

Wilberforce displayed what today we might term a "social conscience," something every civilized society is now expected to have, though in his day it was not simply understood that the right thing to do was to speak up for those who were voiceless. He fought to bring this perspective—and the duty that goes along with it—into his community, and he succeeded. "We had suddenly entered a world in which we would never again ask whether it was our responsibility as a society to help the poor and the suffering."[414] Wilberforce was masterful at engaging people from all walks of life to be a part of something far bigger than themselves.

In 1807, after two decades of unceasing effort on the part of Wilberforce and other abolitionists, "An Act for the Abolition of the Slave Trade" was passed. After passage of the act, Wilberforce continued to support the campaign for the complete abolition of slavery, which would not come about for another twenty-six years. Yet this campaign eventually led to the Slavery Abolition Act of 1833. On his deathbed, Wilberforce received the joyous news that slavery was being abolished throughout the British Empire, and three days later, he died—his life's work accomplished.

I commend Eric Metaxas's stellar biography of Wilberforce to you, *Amazing Grace*. Not only does it provide a wonderful insight into Wilberforce as a man, but it provides an effective blueprint of how to mobilize people to engage a cultural issue in order to right a wrong, restore culture so that it is edifying to all, and protect people of all races, nations, genders, and stages of development.

You come hardwired with useful gifts and talents. Determine how your specific gifts can work to end abortion. Then go do it.

5. Be encouraged and steadfast.

It can be easy to despair or to feel pressured into inaction or silence. Instead, take heart. Press on with confident determination. Know that there are many, many others speaking out, taking a stand, and fighting for those who cannot fight for themselves. Realize that—although the task is monumental and the stakes are nothing short of life and death—there are yet countless reasons to be encouraged and move ahead with the same relentless optimism that William Wilberforce showed in the face of seemingly unbeatable odds:

> Let us not despair; it is a blessed cause, and success, ere long, will crown our exertions . . . let us persevere and our triumph will be complete. Never, never will we desist till we have wiped away this scandal from the Christian name, released ourselves from the load of guilt, under which we at present labour, and extinguished every trace of this bloody traffic, of which our posterity, looking back to the history of these enlightened times, will scarce believe that it has been suffered to exist so long a disgrace and dishonour to this country. (Speech before the House of Commons, April 18, 1791)[415]

Eric Metaxas describes how "[a]bolitionists in the late eighteenth century were something like the characters in horror films who have seen 'the monster' and are trying to tell everyone else about it—and no one believes them."[416] In the same way, we have seen abortion as the "greatest destroyer of love and peace," as Mother Theresa called it. Many in society do not yet believe us, but we know and name the monster for what it is.

We recognize that the aborted children are not the only victims—that millions of mothers, fathers, siblings, and others are victims as well. And we know that abortion exploits the women that it purportedly empowers.

Yet after a long history of wronging women, men today are speaking out and stepping up, serving their spouses and their families and standing their ground on the sanctity of human life. Postabortive men are sharing their stories; fathers are mentoring other men considering abortions for their wives or girlfriends. Others are working to educate the public, spread their testimony, or influence those in positions of power. Men are becoming more involved in their families, their churches, and their cities, and it is making a difference.

I believe that generations in the future will look back upon the struggle to protect preborn life in the same way that generations today regard the fight for the abolition of slavery. Metaxas writes: "From where we stand today—and because of Wilberforce—the end of slavery seems inevitable, and it's impossible for us not to take it largely for granted. But that's the wild miracle of his achievement, that what to the people of his day seemed impossible and unthinkable seems to us, in our day, inevitable."[418]

The end of abortion is neither impossible nor unthinkable.

Be encouraged. Be steadfast.

6. Lead.

While the media, pop culture, aggressive proabortion factions, and extreme feminists continue to attempt to feminize the American male, will you allow those efforts to be successful?

Men, we are built to lead. We fall down; we fail. We've screwed some things up. But we are wired to bounce back, admit our errors, and lead.

This new generation of life-affirming leaders will be different.

We won't lead in order to grab power. We will lead to serve.

We won't lead so that other populations are diminished, controlled, or eliminated. We will lead so that these populations flourish economically, socially, spiritually, and culturally.

We won't treat certain people groups as less equal or valuable than others. Each race, nation, and group has unique, infinite value. Each group is special and is to be protected.

We won't discriminate based on race. We reject eugenics, population control, sterilization, abortion, and all other efforts to diminish minority groups. And we welcome our brothers and sisters from all races to our movement to end abortion in America.

We won't discriminate based on handicap. We find abortion based on birth defect, disease, or genetic abnormality reprehensible. All life is infinitely valuable, even if that life does not match society's definition of value.

We will no longer exploit women for our social or personal gain. We recognize women are equal to men and both have infinite value. We will work for true gender equality, recognizing and educating our nation that abortion, though legal, is inherently immoral and discriminatory. It is undeniably harmful to individual women and the female gender as a whole. It widens the gender gap, essentially lowering women to a tool for misguided social agendas or personal pleasure.

We recognize that abortion is rampant in America because of unplanned pregnancy. Thus we will, as individual men and as a gender, stop engaging in behaviors and actions that cause unplanned pregnancies. We reject pornography, recognizing its direct connection to unwanted pregnancy. We will commit to sexual fidelity with our wives, not only for the benefit of our spouses, but for our families, our communities, and our country. We reject the sexual revolution and its resulting behaviors. We commit to the highest level of sexual integrity and will work aggressively to educate other men to the same.

We commit to a continuum of care for those families facing unplanned pregnancies. Rescuing a baby and family from abortion is not

225

the last step; it is the first. We will work in our communities to identify, establish, promote, and build those services essential for the care of families facing a birth they did not originally anticipate. This includes adoption services for those courageous families who carry a child to term and place the baby into another family.

We will not judge, scorn, or deride our postabortive brothers and sisters. There are too many victims, both born and preborn, to start casting stones. Instead, we welcome those postabortive parents with open arms, commit to helping them heal, and give them an opportunity to rescue another family from their pain and suffering.

We will celebrate, affirm, and protect life at every stage, from conception to natural death.

We reject abortion in totality. There is no rational, moral reason for abortion in America or around the world. Preborn children are the weakest among us, with no voice of their own. They are innocent, having committed no offense against us. They deserve every opportunity to live—not die.

We, as men, recognize and repent of our role in the promotion, legalization, and continuation of abortion in America. We acknowledge it is not hyperbole to say that the very fabric of American life depends on us.

With humility, faithfulness, and relentless perseverance, we commit our time, resources, energy, heart, and testimony to this cause: to end abortion in America.

And we will.

If this book has challenged you, provoked you, and made you righteously angry at the exploitation of women and children at the hands of men, go to www.AbortionExploitsWomen.com to put your anger into proper action.

Resources

This list is by no means exhaustive, and I invite you to look for life-affirming local or national groups that resonate with you.

Share your postabortive stories and honor aborted children:
    AbortionMemorial.com

More information about this book:
    AbortionExploitsWomen.com

For more information about Human Coalition:
    HumanCoalition.org
    Facebook.com/HumanCoalition

Get involved with your local pregnancy resource centers and other compassion organizations:
    EmbraceGrace.org
    Care-Net.org
    HeartbeatInternational.org
    Or search online for the closest life-affirming center in your area.

Find help if you are a postabortive man or woman:
    MenAndAbortion.net
    FatherhoodForever.org
    SurrenderingTheSecret.com
    SilentNoMoreAwareness.org

HopeAfterAbortion.com (Project Rachel)

AfterAbortion.com

Support other life-affirming organizations and efforts:

NRLC.org

40DaysForLife.com

MarchForLife.org

SavetheStorks.com

180Movie.com

SBA-List.org

Support organizations doing life-affirming legal work:

LawofLifeProject.org

AUL.org

ACLJ.org

ADFlegal.org

ThomasMore.org

Endnotes

Introduction

1. *Roe v. Wade*, 410 U.S. 113 (1973), Cornell University Law School, Legal Information Institute, https://www.law.cornell.edu/supremecourt/text/410/113.

2. *Planned Parenthood of Southeastern Pa. v. Casey* (91-744), 505 U.S. 833 (1992), https://www.law.cornell.edu/supremecourt/text/505/833.

3. *Roe v. Wade*, 410 U.S. 113 (1973), Cornell University Law School, Legal Information Institute, https://www.law.cornell.edu/supremecourt/text/410/113.

4. "Unmarried Childbearing," FastStats, Centers for Disease Control, http://www.cdc.gov/nchs/fastats/unmarried-childbearing.htm.

5. US Census Bureau, Table C2: "Household Relationship and Living Arrangements of Children Under 18 Years, by Age and Sex: 2014," http://www.census.gov/hhes/families/data/cps2014C.html.

6. US Census Bureau, Table FG10: "America's Families and Living Arrangements: 2014: Family groups," http://www.census.gov/hhes/families/data/cps2014FG.html.

7. *Roe v. Wade*, 410 U.S. 113 (1973), Cornell University Law School, Legal Information Institute, https://www.law.cornell.edu/supremecourt/text/410/113.

8. Lawrence B. Finer, et al, "Reasons U.S. Women Have Abortions: Quantitative and Qualitative Perspectives," *Perspectives on Sexual and Reproductive Health* 37:3 (2005): 113, https://www.guttmacher.org/pubs/journals/3711005.pdf.

9. M. Antonia Biggs, Heather Gould, and Diana Greene Foster, "Understanding why women seek abortions in the US," *BMC Women's Health* 13:29 (5 July 2013), http://bmcwomenshealth.biomedcentral.com/articles/10.1186/1472-6874-13-29.

10. Kathleen McDonnell, *Not An Easy Choice: Re-Examining Abortion*, (Toronto: Second Story Press, 2003), 59.

11. Connie Schultz, "Sorry, boys, but abortion is a women's issue," *Cleveland Plain Dealer*, Jan. 21, 2008, http://blog.cleveland.com/pdworld/2008/ 01/sorry_boys_but_abortion_is_a_w.html.

12. Cynthia Gorney, *Articles of Faith: A Frontline History of the Abortion Wars* (New York: Simon and Schuster, 2000), 401.

13. Bernard Nathanson, with Richard N. Ostling, *Aborting America* (Garden City, New York: Doubleday, 1979), 171.

14. Cynthia Gorney, *Articles of Faith: A Frontline History of the Abortion Wars* (New York: Simon and Schuster, 2000), 401.

Chapter One

15. "Fastats: Leading Causes of Death," Centers for Disease Control, http://www.cdc.gov/nchs/fastats/lcod.htm, and "U.S. Abortion Statistics," Abort73.com, http://www.abort73.com/abortion_facts/us_abortion_statistics/.

16. "Facts on Induced Abortion in the United States," Guttmacher Institute, Aug. 2011, http://www.guttmacher.org/pubs/fb_induced_abortion.html#4a.

17. "Abortion for Profit," Abort73.com, September 3, 2010, http://www.abort73.com/abortion/abortion_for_profit/.

18. Mark Crutcher, "Baby Body Parts for Sale," LifeDynamics.com, February 2000, updated March 2007, http://www.lifedynamics.com/abortion_information/baby_body_parts/.

19. Barack Obama, "Statement by the President on Roe v. Wade Anniversary," Whitehouse.gov, http://www.whitehouse.gov/the-press-office/2012/01/22/statement-president-roe-v-wade-anniversary.

20. "Mark Ruffalo On Abortion: 'I Don't Want To Turn Back The Hands Of Time,'" Huffingtonpost.com, August 19, 2013, http://www.huffingtonpost.com/2013/08/19/mark-ruffalo-abortion-turn-back-the-hands-of-time_n_3781296.html .

21. "Hillary Clinton on Abortion," OnTheIssues.org, http://www.ontheissues.org/senate/hillary_clinton_abortion.htm.

22. Eddie Vedder, "Reclamation," *Spin Magazine* (Nov. 1992), The Pearl Jam Reference Library, http://www.freewebs.com/pearljamstudy/992spinmagazinereclamati.htm.

23. Jane Fonda, Jane Fonda's Journal, http://janefonda.livejournal.com/.

24. Lily Allen, Tweet, "Can small-minded idiot blokes stop telling women whether or not they're entitled to abortions please? #enoughnow", https://twitter.com/lilyallen/status/255435316683481089.

25. "Sarah Silverman on the Assault on Reproductive Rights," Salon.com, Nov. 19, 2013, http://www.salon.com/2013/11/19/ sarah_silverman_on_the_assault_on_reproductive_rights/.

26. "Michael Bloomberg," Wikipedia.org, The Wikimedia Foundation, http://en.wikipedia.org/wiki/Michael_Bloomberg#cite_ref-99.

27. "A Message from Gwyneth Paltrow and Blythe Danner," http://operationrescue.org/images/dannerpaltrow%20email.pdf.

28. Lucas Neff, Tweet, "A pile of goop should not have more rights than a human being. Period.", https://twitter.com/reallucasneff/status/625781808139874304.

29. "Upcoming Pro-Choice Rally Said to Be the Largest in History," NBC News, April 7, 1989, NBC Universal Archives, http://www.nbcuniversalarchives.com/nbcuni/clip/5112663017_004.do.

30. Deborah Danielski, "Deconstructing the Abortion License," *Our Sunday Visitor* (Oct. 25, 1998).

31. Jan Langman, *Medical Embryology*, 3rd ed. (Baltimore: Williams and Wilkins, 1975), 3.

32. Douglas Considine, ed., *Van Nostrand's Scientific Encyclopedia*, 5th ed. (New York: Van Nostrand Reinhold Company, 1976), 943.

33. F. Beck, *Human Embryology* (Blackwell Scientific Publications, 1985), vi.

34. Keith L. Moore, *Essentials of Human Embryology* (Toronto: B.C. Decker Inc, 1988), 2.

35. Keith L. Moore and T.V.N. Persaud, *Before We Are Born: Essentials of Embryology and Birth Defects*, 4th ed. (Philadelphia: W.B. Saunders Company, 1993), 1.

36. T. W. Sadler, *Langman's Medical Embryology*, 7th ed. (Baltimore: Williams & Wilkins, 1995), 3.

37. Bruce M. Carlson, *Patten's Foundations of Embryology*, 6th ed. (New York: McGraw-Hill, 1996), 3.

38. Keith L. Moore, *The Developing Human: Clinically Oriented Embryology*, 7th ed. (Philadelphia, PA: Saunders, 2003.), 16, 2.

39. Signorelli et al., "Kinases, phosphatases and proteases during sperm capacitation," *Cell Tissue Res.* 349(3):765 (Mar. 20, 2012).

40. National Institutes of Health, *Medline Plus Merriam-Webster Medical Dictionary* (2013), http://www.merriamwebster.com/medlineplus/fertilization

41. Steven Hecht Orzack, et al., "The human sex ratio from conception to birth," *PNAS* (March 30, 2015), http://www.pnas.org/content/112/16/E2102.full.pdf.

42. "Sex-Selection Abortion," House Report 112-496 - PRENATAL NON-DISCRIMINATION ACT (PRENDA) OF 2012, http://thomas.loc.gov/cgi-bin/cpquery/?&sid=cp112SUHud&r_n=hr496.112&dbname=cp112&&sel=TOC_25644&.

43. Abrevaya, Jason, "Are There Missing Girls in the United States? Evidence from Birth Data," *American Economic Journal: Applied Economics*, 1:2 (2009), 1–34, http://www.aeaweb.org/articles.php?doi=10.1257/app.1.2.1.

44. Matthew Jacobs, "Pro-Life Celebrities: Jack Nicholson, Mel Gibson and Other Stars Who Are Anti-Abortion," Huffingtonpost.com, Feb. 1, 2013, http://www.huffingtonpost.com/2013/02/01/pro-life-celebrities_n_2601893.html.

45. Michael W. Chapman, "Jack Nicholson on Abortion," CNSNews.com, Sep. 4, 2013, http://www.cnsnews.com/news/article/michael-w-chapman/jack-nicholson-abortion-i-m-positively-against-it-i-never-would-have.

46. Fred Schruers, "Jack Nicholson: The *Rolling Stone* Interview," *Rolling Stone* (Aug. 14, 1986), http://www.rollingstone.com/culture/features/the-rolling-stone-interview-jack-nicholson-19860814?page=6.

47. Bruce Walker, "Radiance Foundation's Ryan Bomberger: Rape Is No Reason for Abortion," *The New American* (Nov. 11, 2011), http://www.thenewamerican.com/culture/family/item/825-radiance-foundations-ryan-bomberger-rape-is-no-reason-for-abortion.

48. "Roe v. Wade at 40: Most Oppose Overturning Abortion Decision," The Pew Forum on Religion and Public Life, Jan. 16, 2013, http://www.pewforum.org/Abortion/roe-v-wade-at-40.aspx.

49. Quinnipiac University Poll, Nov. 25, 2014, Release Detail, https://www.qu.edu/news-and-events/quinnipiac-university-poll/national/release-detail?ReleaseID=2115.

50. "Roe v. Wade at 40: Most Oppose Overturning Abortion Decision," The Pew Forum on Religion and Public Life, Jan. 16, 2013, http://www.pewforum.org/Abortion/roe-v-wade-at-40.aspx.

51. "Florynce Kennedy Quotes," About Education, http://womenshistory.about.com/od/quotes/a/Florynce-Kennedy-quotes.htm.

52. Scott Klusendorf, *The Case for Life: Equipping Christians to Engage the Culture* (Wheaton, Ill.: Crossway Books, 2009), 182–3.

53. Dr. Keith Ablow, "Men Should Be Allowed to Veto Abortions," Foxnews.com, July 22, 2011, http://www.foxnews.com/opinion/2011/07/22/men-should-be-allowed-to-veto-abortions/#ixzz2IeIii0fe.

54. David Bereit and Shawn Carney, *40 Days for Life* (Nashville: Capella Books, 2013) 106–8.

55. Phil McCombs, "Remembering Thomas," *Washington Post*, Feb. 3, 1995. http://www.priestsforlife.org/postabortion/rememberingthomas.htm.

Chapter Two

56. *Scott v. Sanford*, 60 U.S. (19 How.) 393 (1857).

57. *Roe v. Wade*, 410 U.S. 113 (1973), Cornell University Law School, Legal Information Institute, https://www.law.cornell.edu/supremecourt/text/410/113.

58. Ibid.

59. Ibid.

60. Randall O'Bannon, "Why Do Women Have Abortions? New Study Provides Some Answers," Oct. 10, 2013, Lifenews.com, http://www.lifenews.com/2013/10/10/why-do-women-have-abortions-new-study-provides-some-answers/.

61. Serrin Foster, "Pro-Woman Answers to Pro-Choice Questions," Feminists for Life, http://www.feministsforlife.org/can-you-really-be-a-feminist-and-pro-life/.

62. *Roe v. Wade*, 410 U.S. 113 (1973), Cornell University Law School, Legal Information Institute, https://www.law.cornell.edu/supremecourt/text/410/113.

63. "Summary of Vital Statistics 2013. The City of New York Pregnancy Outcomes," New York City Dept. of Health and Mental Hygiene, Feb. 2015, http://www.nyc.gov/html/doh/downloads/pdf/vs/vs-pregnancy-outcomes-2013.pdf.

64. Jaime L Natoli, et al., "Prenatal Diagnosis of Down Syndrome: A Systematic Review of Termination Rates (1995–2011)," *Prenat. Diagn.* 32 (2012): 142–53,http://onlinelibrary.wiley.com/doi/10.1002/pd.2910/epdf.

65. *Roe v. Wade*, 410 U.S. 113 (1973), Cornell University Law School, Legal Information Institute, https://www.law.cornell.edu/supremecourt/text/410/113.

66. Ibid.

67. Moore and Persaud, *The Developing Human: Clinically Oriented Embryology*, 5th ed. (Saunders Company, 1993), 1.

68. *Roe v. Wade*, 410 U.S. 113 (1973), Cornell University Law School, Legal Information Institute, https://www.law.cornell.edu/supremecourt/text/410/113.

69. Report, Subcommittee on Separation of Powers to Senate Judiciary Committee S-158, 97th Cong., 1st Sess., 1981. Quoted in Randy Alcorn, *ProLife Answers to ProChoice Arguments* (Colorado Springs: Multnomah Books, 2000), 53.

70. Ibid.

71. Ibid.

72. Report, Subcommittee on Separation of Powers to Senate Judiciary Committee S-158, 97th Cong., 1st Sess., 1981, 7. Quoted in Randy Alcorn, *ProLife Answers to ProChoice Arguments* (Colorado Springs: Multnomah Books, 2000), 55.

73. *Planned Parenthood v. Casey,* 505 U.S. 833 (1992), Cornell University Law School, Legal Information Institute, https://www.law.cornell.edu/supct/html/91-744.ZS.html.

74. Timothy Keller, *The Reason for God: Belief in an Age of Skepticism* (New York: Dutton, 2008), 36 n3.

75. *Roe v. Wade,* 410 U.S. 113 (1973), Cornell University Law School, Legal Information Institute, https://www.law.cornell.edu/supremecourt/text/410/113.

76. Randy Alcorn, *ProLife Answers to ProChoice Arguments* (Colorado Springs: Multnomah Books, 2000), 57–103.

77. Ibid., 80.

78. *Doe v. Bolton* 410 U.S. 179 (1973), Cornell University Law School, Legal Information Institute, https://www.law.cornell.edu/supremecourt/text/410/179.

79. *Thornburgh v. American College of Obstetricians and Gynecologists* 476 U.S. 747 (1986), Cornell University Law School, Legal Information Institute, https://www.law.cornell.edu/supremecourt/text/476/747.

80. Text of an E-Mail from Sen. John Kerry (D-Ma.) on the Unborn Victims of Violence Act, June 27, 2003, http://www.nrlc.org/Unborn_Victims/kerrye-mailUVVA.html.

81. "Fetal Homicide Laws," National Conference of State Legislatures, http://www.ncsl.org/research/health/fetal-homicide-state-laws.aspx.

82. Nina Martin, "This Alabama Judge Has Figured Out How to Dismantle Roe v. Wade," Oct. 10, 2014, ProPublica, https://www.propublica.org/article/this-alabama-judge-has-figured-out-how-to-dismantle-roe-v-wade.

Chapter Three

83. From *Lysistrata*, quoted in Alvin J. Schmidt, *How Christianity Changed the World* (Grand Rapids, Michigan: Zondervan, 2001, 2004), 98.

84. Alvin J. Schmidt, *How Christianity Changed the World* (Grand Rapids, Michigan: Zondervan, 2001, 2004), 97–101.

85. David H. Cherry, ed., *The Roman World: A Sourcebook* (Malden, Mass: Blackwell Publishers, 2001), 51.

86. Philip Schaff, *The Person of Christ: The Miracle of History* (Boston: American Tract Society, 1865.), 210. Cited in Alvin J. Schmidt, *How Christianity Changed the World* (Grand Rapids, Michigan: Zondervan, 2001, 2004), 101.

87. Talmud, Sotah, 19a, Cited in Gary R. Habermas and Michael L. Licona, *The Case for the Resurrection of Jesus* (Grand Rapids, Michigan: Kregel Publications, 2004), 72.

88. Gary R. Habermas and Michael L. Licona, *The Case for the Resurrection of Jesus* (Grand Rapids, Michigan: Kregel Publications, 2004), 72.

89. Sakuntala Narasimhan, *Sati: Widow Burning in India* (New York: Anchor Books, 1990), 27.

90. Dorothy K. Stein, "Women to Burn: Suttee as a Normative Institution," *Signs: Journal of Women Culture and Society* (Winter 1978), 253. Cited in Schmidt, *How Christianity Changed the World*, 116.

91. Alvin J. Schmidt, *How Christianity Changed the World* (Grand Rapids, Michigan: Zondervan, 2001, 2004), 118–9.

92. Alexis de Tocqueville, *Democracy in America* (London: Saunders and Otley, 1840), 106.

93. Modern History Sourcebook: The Declaration of Sentiments, Seneca Falls Conference, 1848, http://www.fordham.edu/halsall/mod/senecafalls.asp.

94. Nonie Darwish, *Cruel and Usual Punishment* (Nashville: Thomas Nelson, 2008), 64.

95. Ibid., ix.

96. Farid Ahmed and Moni Basu, "Only 14, Bangladeshi girl charged with adultery was lashed to death," CNN.com, March 29, 2011, http://edition.cnn.com/2011/WORLD/asiapcf/03/29/bangladesh.lashing.death/index.html.

97. Sabina Amidi, "I wed Iranian girls before execution," *The Jerusalem Post*, July 19, 2009, http://www.jpost.com/IranianThreat/News/Article.aspx?id=149091.

98. "Rifqa Bary Granted U.S. Residency," 10TV.com, September 7, 2010, http://www.10tv.com/content/stories/2010/09/07/story-columbus-rifqa-bary-us-citizen-granted.html.

99. Julia Dahl, "'Honor killing' under growing scrutiny in the U.S.," CBSNews.com, April 4, 2012, http://www.cbsnews.com/8301-504083_162-57409395-504083/honor-killing-under-growing-scrutiny-in-the-u.s/.

100. Preeti, "Wars and Bars: Women in Iraq," Jan. 15, 2014, Fair Observer, http://www.fairobserver.com/region/middle_east_north_africa/wars-bars-women-iraq/.

101. "Ten Worst Countries for Women," The Star, Mar. 8, 2008, http://www.thestar.com/news/world/2008/03/08/ten_worst_countries_for_women.html.

102. Ibid.

103. Jeffrey Gettleman, "The World's Worst War," *New York Times*, Sunday Review, Dec. 15, 2012, http://www.nytimes.com/2012/12/16/sunday-review/congos-never-ending-war.html?_r=0.

104. "Ten Worst Countries for Women," The Star, Mar. 8, 2008, http://www.thestar.com/news/world/2008/03/08/ten_worst_countries_for_women.html.

105. Justin Lynch, "Women Are Sex Slaves in South Sudan's Civil War," Mar. 13, 2016, The Daily Beast, http://www.thedailybeast.com/articles/2016/03/14/women-are-sex-slaves-in-south-sudan-s-civil-war.html.

106. "Ten Worst Countries for Women," The Star, Mar. 8, 2008, http://www.thestar.com/news/world/2008/03/08/ten_worst_countries_for_women.html.

107. "Women, Peace and Security," Amnesty International USA, http://www.amnestyusa.org/our-work/issues/women-s-rights/women-peace-and-security.

108. "Women in Parliament in 2011: The Year in Perspective," Inter-Parliamentary Union, http://www.ipu.org/pdf/publications/wmnpersp11-e.pdf.

109. "Human Rights Violation," United Nations Secretary-General's Campaign, UNiTE To End Violence Against Women, http://endviolence.un.org/situation.shtml.

110. Ibid.

Chapter Four

111. *National Crime Victimization Survey*, 2009–2013, US Department of Justice.

112. "Victims sex by offense category," Federal Bureau of Investigation, 2012. "Offenders sex by offense category," Federal Bureau of Investigation, 2012.

113. Dean G. Kilpatrick, "Drug-facilitated, Incapacitated, and Forcible Rape: A National Study," July 2007, National Criminal Justice Reference Service, United States Department of Justice, 43–45.

114. *National Crime Victimization Survey*, 2008–2012, US Department of Justice; see also National Research Council, *Estimating the Incidence of Rape and Sexual Assault* (Washington, DC: The National Academies Press, 2013).

115. C. R. Yung, "How to Lie with Rape Statistics: America's Hidden Rape Crisis," *Iowa Law Review* 99 (2014), 1197.

116. *National Crime Victimization Survey*, 2008–2012, US Department of Justice.

117. "The Facts," The Polaris Project, https://polarisproject.org/facts.

118. "UN senior officials urge countries to boost their efforts to combat human trafficking," April 3, 2012, UN News Centre, http://www.un.org/apps/news/story.asp?NewsID=41696#.VvVqjuIrKt-.

119. 2014 Global Slavery Index, The Global Slavery Index, http://www.globalslaveryindex.org/.

120. "United States of America," HumanTrafficking.org, http://www.humantrafficking.org/countries/united_states_of_america.

121. "The Facts," The Polaris Project, https://polarisproject.org/facts.

122. Eleanor Goldberg, "10 Things You Didn't Know About Slavery, Human Trafficking (And What You Can Do About It)," Jan. 15, 2014, *The Huffington Post*, http://www.huffingtonpost.com/2014/01/15/human-trafficking-month_n_4590587.html.

123. Mary Eberstadt and Mary Anne Layden, "The Social Costs of Pornography: A Statement of Findings and Recommendations," The Witherspoon Institute and the Social Trends Institute, 2010, p. 35, http://www.internetsafety101.org/upload/file/Social%20Costs%20of%20Pornography%20Report.pdf.

124. Ibid., 25.

125. Mary Anne Layden, Center for Cognitive Therapy, Department of Psychiatry, University of Pennsylvania, Testimony for US Senate Committee on Commerce, Science and Transportation, November 18, 2004, 2.

126. John D. Foubert, Matt W. Brosi, and R Sean Bannon, "Pornography viewing among fraternity men: Effects on bystander intervention, rape myth acceptance and behavioral intent to commit sexual assault," *Journal of Sex Addiction and Compulsivity* 18 (2011): 212–31, http://works.bepress.com/john_foubert/7.

127. "Fatal Addiction: Ted Bundy's Final Interview," PureIntimacy.org, http://www.pureintimacy.org/piArticles/A000000433.cfm.

128. Michael L. Bourke and Andres E. Hernandez, "The 'Butner Study' Redux: A Report of Incidence of Hands-on Child Victimization by Child Pornography Offenders," *Journal of Family Violence* 24 (2009): 183–91 (187).

129. Eleanor Goldberg, "10 Things You Didn't Know About Slavery, Human Trafficking (And What You Can Do About It)," Jan. 15, 2014, *The Huffington Post*, http://www.huffingtonpost.com/2014/01/15/human-trafficking-month_n_4590587.html.

130. Ellie Hamalian, "How Pornography Fuels Exploitation," Nov. 19, 2014, *The Huffington Post*, http://www.huffingtonpost.com/ellie-hamalian/how-pornography-fuels-exp_b_6187936.html.

131. Julie Bindel, "The truth about the porn industry," July 2, 2010, *The Guardian*, http://www.theguardian.com/lifeandstyle/2010/jul/02/gail-dines-pornography.

132. Wil S. Hylton, "Hugh Hefner: What I've Learned," Jan. 29, 2007, *Esquire*, http://www.esquire.com/entertainment/interviews/a1229/esq0602-jun-wil/.

133. Mary Rose Somarriba, "The Porn Industry Is Abusive, and These Women Are Telling It Like It Is," Aug. 5, 2015, Verily, http://verilymag.com/2015/08/porn-industry-playboy-mansion-sex-trafficking-belle-knox-rashida-jones-holly-madison.

134. Ibid.

135. Mike Allen, Dave D'Alessio, and Keri Brezgel, "A Meta-Analysis Summarizing the Effects of Pornography / Aggression After Exposure," *Human Communication Research* 22:2 (Dec. 1995), 258–83.

136. Donnerstein and Linz, 1998; Malamuth, Addison, and Koss, 2001.

137. Elizabeth Oddone Paolucci, Mark Genuis, and Claudio Violato, "A Meta-Analysis of the Published Research on the Effects of Pornography," National Foundation for Family Research and Education, Calgary, Alberta, https://www.researchgate.net/profile/Claudio_Violato/publication/252364943_A_Meta-Analysis_of_the_Published_Research_on_the_Effects_of_ Pornography/links/0c960531cb31e0e710000000.pdf.

Chapter Five

138. Edwin M. Hale, *The Great Crime of the Nineteenth Century* (Chicago: C.S. Halsey, 1867). Available at http://archive.org/stream/ greatcrimeofnine-00hale/greatcrimeofnine00hale_djvu.txt.

139. Marvin Olasky, *Abortion Rites: A Social History of Abortion in America* (Wheaton, Illinois: Crossway Books, 1992), 291.

140. A. K., Gardner, "Physical Decline of American Women," Health Reformer, September 1876. In *Good Health*, Vol. 11 (Good Health Publishing Company, 1876), 259.

141. Marvin Olasky, *Abortion Rites: A Social History of Abortion in America* (Wheaton, Illinois: Crossway Books, 1992), 22.

142. Ibid., 102.

143. Serrin Foster, "How Men Convinced Women to be Pro-Abortion," Catholic-Culture.org, http://www.catholicculture.org/culture/library/view.cfm?recnum=111.

144. Elizabeth Cady Stanton, *The Revolution*, February 5 and March 12, 1868.

145. "Herstory Worth Repeating," Feminists for Life, http://www.feministsforlife.org/herstory/.

146. Mary Ann Glendon, "The Women of Roe v. Wade," First Things, June/July 2003, http://www.firstthings.com/article/2007/01/the-women-of-roe-v-wade-34.

147. Susan B. Anthony, *The Revolution*, July 8, 1869. Emphasis added.

148. "Alice Paul" entry in *New World Encyclopedia*, http://www.newworldencyclopedia.org/entry/Alice_Paul.

149. Ibid.

150. Kate O'Beirne, "Pro-Life Women Fight For Feminism," NationalReview.com, January 23, 2006, http://www.nationalreview.com/articles/216565/pro-life-women-fight-feminism/kate-obeirne.

151. *McDowall's Journal*, May 1833, p. 36. Quoted in Marvin Olasky, *Abortion Rites: A Social History of Abortion in America* (Wheaton, Illinois: Crossway Books, 1992), 141.

152. Ibid., April 1834, 31. Quoted in Olasky, 142.

153. *National Police Gazette*, February 14, 1846, 205. Quoted in Marvin Olasky, *Abortion Rites: A Social History of Abortion in America* (Wheaton, Illinois: Crossway Books, 1992), 149.

154. "The Evil of the Age," *New York Times*, August 23, 1871. Cited in Marvin Olasky, *Abortion Rites: A Social History of Abortion in America* (Wheaton, Illinois: Crossway Books, 1992), 153.

155. AMA Report on Criminal Abortion, 1859, http://www.abortionessay.com files/1859ama.html.

156. Frederick N. Dyer, "How Abortion Became Illegal in the United States," Patheos.com, May 25, 2011, http://www.patheos.com/Resources/Additional-Resources/How-Abortion-Became-Illegal-in-the-United-States-Frederick-Dyer-05-25-2011.html.

157. H. R. Storer, "Criminal Abortion: Its Prevalence, Its Prevention, and Its Relation to the Medical Examiner . . . ," Microfiche #AN 0320 in the Adelaide Nutting Historical Nursing Microfilm Collection; microfiche of an offprint of the article in *Atlantic Medical Weekly* 1897, 209–18. Offprint page numbers 1–34, p. 12–13. Cited by Frederick Dyer in "John Preston Leonard's 'Quackery and

Abortion': Blueprint for Horatio Robinson Storer's Crusade Against Abortion?" http://horatiostorer.net/Quackery_and__Abortion.html#_ednref10.

158. Joseph Meredith Toner, *Transactions of the American Medical Association*, Vol. 16 (Philadelphia: Collins Printer, 1866), 723.

159. Frederick N. Dyer, "How Abortion Became Illegal in the United States," Patheos.com, May 25, 2011, http://www.patheos.com/Resources/Additional-Resources/How-Abortion-Became-Illegal-in-the-United-States-Frederick-Dyer-05-25-2011.html.

160. James Mohr, *Abortion in America* (New York: Oxford University Press, 1978), 240. Cited in Marvin Olasky, *Abortion Rites: A Social History of Abortion in America* (Wheaton, Illinois: Crossway Books, 1992), 198.

161. *Journal of the American Medical Association*, Vol. 46 (April 28, 1909), 1309. Cited in Marvin Olasky, *Abortion Rites: A Social History of Abortion in America* (Wheaton, Illinois: Crossway Books, 1992), 194.

162. Marvin Olasky, *Abortion Rites: A Social History of Abortion in America* (Wheaton, Illinois: Crossway Books, 1992), 194–6.

163. Minutes of the Chicago Medical Society, Vol. 17, October 1905–June 1907. Cited in Marvin Olasky, *Abortion Rites: A Social History of Abortion in America* (Wheaton, Illinois: Crossway Books, 1992), 196.

164. Henry Marcy, "Education as a Factor in the Prevention of Criminal Abortion and Illegitimacy," *Journal of the American Medical Association*, Vol. 47 (1906, 1889). Cited in Marvin Olasky, *Abortion Rites: A Social History of Abortion in America* (Wheaton, Illinois: Crossway Books, 1992), 234–5.

165. Marvin Olasky, *Abortion Rites: A Social History of Abortion in America* (Wheaton, Illinois: Crossway Books, 1992), 235.

166. "Medicine: Abortions," Time, March 16, 1936, http://www.time.com/time/magazine/article/0,9171,755930,00.html.

167. Frederick J. Taussig, *Abortion: Spontaneous and Induced: Medical and Social Aspects* (St. Louis: Mosby, 1936), 448. Cited in Marvin Olasky, *Abortion Rites: A Social History of Abortion in America* (Wheaton, Illinois: Crossway Books, 1992), 261.

168. Taussig, *Abortion*, 390. Cited in Samuel W. Calhoun, "Sowing the Wind, Reaping the Whirlwind: From Frederick Taussig's *Abortion: Spontaneous and Induced* (1936) to Warren Hern's *Abortion Practice* (1984)," http://uffl.org/vol10/calhoun10.pdf.

169. *The Abortion Problem* (The Williams & Wilkins Co., 1944, publishing the proceedings of a 1942 conference), 28. Cited in Samuel W. Calhoun, "Sowing the Wind, Reaping the Whirlwind: From Frederick Taussig's *Abortion: Spontaneous and Induced* (1936) to Warren Hern's *Abortion Practice* (1984)." http://uffl.org/vol10/calhoun10.pdf.

170. Mary Calderone, "Illegal Abortion as a Public Health Problem," *American Journal of Public Health*, 50:7, 949. http://www.ncbi.nlm.nih.gov/pmc/articles/PMC1373382/pdf/amjphnation00308-0022.pdf.

171. The Abortion Problem: Proceedings of the Conference Held Under the Auspices of the National Committee on Maternal Health, Inc. (Baltimore: Wil-

liams and Wilkins, 1944) 50–2, 104. Cited in Marvin Olasky, *Abortion Rites: A Social History of Abortion in America* (Wheaton, Illinois: Crossway Books, 1992), 262.

172. Mary Calderone, ed., *Abortion in the United States* (New York: Hoeber-Harper, 1958), 166. Cited in Marvin Olasky, *Abortion Rites: A Social History of Abortion in America* (Wheaton, Illinois: Crossway Books, 1992), 263.

173. Ibid., 109. Cited in Olasky, 263.

174. Marvin Olasky, *Abortion Rites: A Social History of Abortion in America* (Wheaton, Illinois: Crossway Books, 1992), 273.

175. Atlantic Constitution, August 18, 1962, 30. Cited in Marvin Olasky, *Abortion Rites: A Social History of Abortion in America* (Wheaton, Illinois: Crossway Books, 1992), 280.

176. *The Gallup Poll, Public Opinion 1935–1971* (New York: Random House, 1972), 1984. Cited in Marvin Olasky, *Abortion Rites: A Social History of Abortion in America* (Wheaton, Illinois: Crossway Books, 1992), 281.

177. "The Cruel Abortion Law," *New York Times*, April 7, 1965.

178. Leslie J. Reagan, *When Abortion Was a Crime: Women, Medicine, and Law in the United States, 1867–1973* (Berkeley, Calif.: University of California Press, 1997), 222, see note 15 for list of states. Also see Sarah Kliff, "CHARTS: How Roe v. Wade changed abortion rights," WashingtonPost.com, January 22, 2013, http://www.washingtonpost.com/blogs/wonkblog/wp/2013/01/22/charts-how-roe-v-wade-changed-abortion-rights/.

179. Douglas Martin, "Lawrence Lader, Champion of Abortion Rights, Is Dead at 86," *New York Times*, May 10, 2006, http://www.nytimes.com/2006/05/10/nyregion/10lader.html?_r=1&.

180. Bernard Nathanson, *The Hand of God* (Washington, D.C.: Regnery, 1996), 86.

181. Bernard Nathanson, with Richard N. Ostling, *Aborting America* (Garden City, New York: Doubleday, 1979), 31.

182. Elaine Woo, "Lawrence Lader, 86; Activist for Abortion Rights Whose Book Was Cited in Roe Case," *Los Angeles Times*, May 14, 2006, http://articles.latimes.com/2006/may/14/local/me-lader14.

183. Margaret Sanger, *Woman and the New Race* (New York: Truth Publishing Co., 1920), 94. Quoted in Lawrence Lader, *Abortion II: Making the Revolution* (Boston: Beacon Press, 1974), 18.

184. Lawrence Lader, *Abortion II: Making the Revolution* (Boston: Beacon Press, 1974), ix.

185. Ibid.

186. David J. Garrow, *Liberty and Sexuality: The Right to Privacy and the Making of Roe v. Wade* (Berkeley, Calif.: University of California Press, 1994), 292.

187. Bernard Nathanson, with Richard N. Ostling, *Aborting America* (Garden City, New York: Doubleday, 1979), 32.

188. Ibid., 32–33.

189. Ibid., 50.

190. Ibid., 53.

191. Ibid.
192. Bernard Nathanson, *The Hand of God* (Washington, D.C.: Regnery Gateway, 1996), 88.
193. Rosemary Oelrich Bottcher, "Men Launched the Movement to Legalize Abortion," FeministsforLife.org, http://feministsforlife.org/news/men-launched-the-movement-to-legalize-abortion.htm.
194. Betty Friedan, *Life So Far: A Memoir* (New York: Simon & Schuster), 377.
195. Betty Friedan, *The Second Stage: With a New Introduction* (Cambridge, Mass.: Harvard Univ. Press, 1981, 1986, 1991, 1998), 246–8, esp. 247.
196. Stella Morabito, "Feminist enablers of the war against women," *Washington Examiner*, March 11, 2012, http://washingtonexaminer.com/feminist-enablers-of-the-war-against-women/article/361536#.UQQ6efL9V8M.
197. Judith Blake, "Abortion and Public Opinion: The 1960–1970 Decade," 1971. Cited in Eva R. Rubin, editor, *The Abortion Controversy: A Documentary History* (Westport, Conn.: 1994), 107.
198. Edward Manier, William Thomas Liu, W. D. Solomon, *Abortion: New Direction for Policy Studies* (University of Notre Dame Press, 1977), 7.
199. Interview with Bernard Nathanson, M.D., 1986. Miriam Claire, *Abortion Dilemma: Personal Views on a Public Issue* (New York: Insight Books, 1995), 127. Cited on http://clinicquotes.com/dr-bernard-nathanson-on-abortion/.

Chapter Six

200. Jeremy Carl, "China's Children and Climate Change: The Left Is against Them Both," Nov. 2, 2015, National Review, http://www.nationalreview.com/article/426458/chinas-children-and-climate-change-left-against-them-both-jeremy-carl.
201. Ibid.
202. Reggie Littlejohn, "China's Two-Child Policy, New Number – Same Violence against Women," Dec. 3, 2015, Women's Rights Without Frontiers, Congressional-Executive Commission on China, http://www.womensrightswithoutfrontiers.org/blog/?p=2130.
203. Ibid.
204. Nancy Flanders, "Under China's Two-Child Policy, There Will Still Be 'hundreds of women crying each day,'" Nov. 4, 2015, LifeSite, https://www.lifesitenews.com/opinion/under-chinas-two-child-policy-there-will-still-be-hundreds-of-women-crying.
205. Jeremy Carl, "China's Children and Climate Change: The Left Is against Them Both," Nov. 2, 2015, National Review, http://www.nationalreview.com/article/426458/chinas-children-and-climate-change-left-against-them-both-jeremy-carl.
206. Mary Meehan, "How Eugenics and Population Control Led to Abortion," MeehanReports.com. The article originally appeared under the title "The Road to Abortion" as a two-part series in *Human Life Review*, Fall 1998 & Winter 1999. See http://www.meehanreports.com/how-led.html.

207. Adolf Meyer, ed., *Birth control: facts and responsibilities* (The Williams & Wilkins company, 1925), 48.

208. Margaret Sanger, *The Pivot of Civilization* (New York: Brentano's, 1922), Kindle Location 866.

209. Ibid., Kindle Locations 284–6.

210. Lothrop Stoddard, *The Rising Tide of Color Against White World-Supremacy* (New York: Charles Scribner's Son, 1921), vi.

211. "Harry H. Laughlin," Wikipedia.org, the Wikimedia Foundation, https://en.wikipedia.org/wiki/Harry_H._Laughlin.

212. "Eugenics and Euthanasia Quotations in Modern Times," World Future Fund, http://www.worldfuturefund.org/wffmaster/Reading/Biology/Eugenics.htm.

213. Ibid.

214. Ibid.

215. Madeline Gray, *Margaret Sanger: A Biography of the Champion of Birth Control* (New York, Richard Marek Publishers, 1979), 91.

216. Havelock Ellis, Spartacus Educational, http://www.spartacus.schoolnet.co.uk/TUhavelock.htm.

217. George Grant, *Grand Illusions: The Legacy of Planned Parenthood* (Nashville: Cumberland House Publishing, 1988), 115.

218. Havelock Ellis, "The Sterilization of the Unfit," *Eugenics Review*, October 1909, 203–6. http://www.ncbi.nlm.nih.gov/pmc/articles/PMC2986668/?page=1.

219. Havelock Ellis, *The Task of Social Hygiene* (Boston and New York: Houghton Mifflin Company, 1913), 200.

220. Havelock Ellis, *The Problem of Race Regeneration* (London, New York: Cassell and Company, 1911), 67, 69.

221. Madeline Gray, *Margaret Sanger: A Biography of the Champion of Birth Control* (New York, Richard Marek Publishers, 1979), caption on unnumbered photo page.

222. Margaret Sanger, "Let's Talk It Over," 17 July 1939, The Public Writings and Speeches of Margaret Sanger, http://www.nyu.edu/projects/sanger/webedition/app/documents/show.php?sangerDoc=129007.xml.

223. Ibid.

224. Ibid.

225. John Hunt, "Perfecting Humankind: A Comparison of Progressive and Nazi Views on Eugenics, Sterilization, and Abortion," *The Linacre Quarterly* 66:1 (February), 30.

226. The Woman Rebel 1:1 (March 1914), http://wyatt.elasticbeanstalk.com/mep/MS/xml/b3083963.html#b3083963.

227. Margaret Sanger, Family Limitation, pamphlet, 1914, 5, http://library.lifedynamics.com/Family%20Limitation/Family%20Limitation.pdf.

228. Madeline Gray, *Margaret Sanger: A Biography of the Champion of Birth Control* (New York, Richard Marek Publishers, 1979), 159, 280; Also see George Grant, *Grand Illusions: The Legacy of Planned Parenthood* (Nashville: Cumberland House Publishing, 1988, 1992, 1998, 2000), 77.

229. Margaret Sanger, *An Autobiography* (New York: W. W. Norton, 1938), 185.

230. Ibid., 188.

231. Ibid., 217.

232. Robert Marshall and Charles Donovan, *Blessed are the Barren: The Social Policy of Planned Parenthood* (San Francisco: Ignatius Press, 1991), 280.

233. Ibid., 280.

234. Matthew James Connelly, *Fatal Misconception: The Struggle to Control World Population* (Cambridge, Mass.: Harvard University, 2008), 163.

235. Quoted in David J. Garrow, *Liberty and Sexuality: The Right to Privacy and the Making of Roe v. Wade* (Berkeley, Los Angeles: University of California Press, 1994, 1998), 271.

236. Alan Guttmacher, "The Genesis of Liberalized Abortion in New York: A Personal Insight," *Case Western Reserve Law Review* 23 (1972): 756–78. Quoted in Robert Marshall and Charles Donovan, Blessed *Are the Barren: The Social Policy of Planned Parenthood* (San Francisco: Ignatius Press, 1991), 258.

237. "Compulsory Population Control Foreseen," *Medical World News*, June 6, 1969, 11. Quoted in Robert Marshall and Charles Donovan, *Blessed Are the Barren: The Social Policy of Planned Parenthood* (San Francisco: Ignatius Press, 1991), 319.

238. William Stump, "Dr. Guttmacher - Still Optimistic About the Population Problem," *Baltimore Magazine* 63:2 (Feb. 1970), 51–2. Quoted in Mary Meehan, "How Eugenics and Population Control Led to Abortion," MeehanReports.com, http://www.meehanreports.com/how-led.html.

239. Frederick Osborn to P. R. U. Stratton, Jan. 12, 1966, AES Archives, folder on "Osborn, Frederick, Letters on Eugenics." Quoted in Mary Meehan, "How Eugenics and Population Control Led to Abortion," MeehanReports.com, http://www.meehanreports.com/how-led.html.

240. Mary Meehan, "How Eugenics and Population Control Led to Abortion," MeehanReports.com, http://www.meehanreports.com/how-led.html.

241. Frederick Osborn, "Notes on Markle and Fox . . . ," Jan. 25, 1974, Osborn Papers, folder on "Osborn - Paper - Notes on 'Paradigms or Public Relations . . . '" Quoted in Mary Meehan, "How Eugenics and Population Control Led to Abortion," MeehanReports.com, http://www.meehanreports.com/how-led.html.

242. Paul Ehrlich, *The Population Bomb* (New York: Ballantine Books, 1968) 148.

243. Mary Meehan, "How Eugenics and Population Control Led to Abortion," MeehanReports.com, http://www.meehanreports.com/how-led.html.

244. Francis Galton, "Eugenics: Its Definition, Scope and Aims," Nature, 70:1804 (May 26, 1904), 82. Galton.org, http://galton.org/cgi-bin/searchImages/search/essays/pages/galton-1905-socpapers-eugenics-definition-scope-aims_1.htm.

245. Madison Grant, *The Passing of the Great Race: Or, The Racial Basis of European History* (New York: Charles Scribner's Sons, 1922), 60.

246. Gunnar Myrdal, *American Dilemma: The Negro Problem and Modern Democracy*, Vol. 1 (New Brunswick, New Jersey: Transaction Publishers, 1996), 168.

247. Ibid., 170.

248. Ibid., 176.

249. Letter from Margaret Sanger to Dr. Clarence J. Gamble, 225 Adams St., Milton, Mass., December 10, 1939. Quoted in Robert Marshall and Charles Donovan, *Blessed are the Barren: The Social Policy of Planned Parenthood* (San Francisco: Ignatius Press, 1991), 18.

250. Gamble memo, undated but probably November or December 1939, Sanger Collection, Smith College. Cited in Linda Gordon, *Women's Body, Women's Right: Birth Control in America* (New York: Penguin Books, 1990), 329. Also quoted in James Miller, "Betting with lives: Clarence Gamble and the Pathfinder International," *PRI Review* 6:4 (July/August 1996), http://www.pop.org/content/betting-with-lives-clarence-gamble-1752#endnote_anchor-21.

251. Table 12, "Abortion Surveillance — United States, 2009 Surveillance Summaries," November 23, 2012, http://www.cdc.gov/mmwr/preview/mmwrhtml/ss6108a1.htm?s_cid=ss6108a1_w#Tab12.

252. Susan Enouen, "Why Are Black Women Three Times More Likely to Have an Abortion?" LifeNews.com, October 21, 2012, http://www.lifenews.com/2012/10/21/why-are-black-women-three-times-more-likely-to-have-an-abortion/.

253. Mark Crutcher, "Racial Targeting and Population Control," Life Dynamics Incorporated, http://lifenews.wpengine.netdna-cdn.com/wp-content/uploads/2011/08/LifeDynamicsRacialReport.pdf.

254. Jeff Wise, "About That Overpopulation Problem," Slate.com, January 9, 2013, http://www.slate.com/articles/technology/future_tense/2013/01/world_population_may_actually_start_declining_not_exploding.html.

255. Mary Meehan, "The 'Billionaire Brigade' of Population Controllers," MeehanReports.com, http://www.meehanreports.com/billionaire.html.

256. "Secret billionaire club seeks population control," WorldNetDaily.com, June 24, 2009, http://www.wnd.com/2009/05/99105/#mkfemP5JG7MuqYbb.99.

257. "Population," "Eugenics," Merriam-Webster, http://www.merriam-webster.com.

258. Meaghan Parker, "Clinton, Congress Link Family Planning, Climate Change," July 24, 2009, NewSecurityBeat, https://www.newsecuritybeat.org/ 2009/07/clinton-congress-link-family-planning-climate-change/.

259. Patrick Goodenough, "Chinese Minister Links 'One-Child' Policy to Emissions Reduction at Climate Conference," Dec. 11, 2009. CNSNews.com, http://cnsnews.com/news/article/chinese-minister-links-one-child-policy-emissions-reduction-climate-conference.

260. Julie Makinen, "Here's why China is abolishing its one-child policy," Oct. 29, 2015, *Los Angeles Times*, http://www.latimes.com/world/asia/la-fg-why-china-end-one-child-policy20151029-htmlstory.html.

261. Jonathan V. Last, "America's Baby Bust," Feb. 12, 2013, *Wall Street Journal*, http://www.wsj.com/articles/SB10001424127887323375204578270053387770718.

262. Ibid.

263. "Table of Abuses and Violations by Country," Population Research Institute, http://www.pop.org/content/table-abuses-country.

264. "Post documents Indian horror," Population Research Institute, PRI Review, September/October 1997, http://www.pop.org/content/post-documents-indian-horror-1597.

265. Molly Moore, "Teeming India Engulfed by Soaring Birthrate; Sterilization Quotas Blasted As Inhuman and Coercive," *Washington Post*, August 21, 1994.

266. Carol Kuruvilla, "Horror in a mass sterilization camp: Unconscious Indian women were dumped in a field after undergoing a painful sterilization operation," *New York Daily News*, February 7, 2013, http://www.nydailynews.com/news/national/indian-women-dumped-field-sterilization-operation-article-1.1258314.

267. Rafael Romo, "Peruvian authorities reopen investigation into forced sterilizations," CNN.com, November 17, 2011, http://www.cnn.com/2011/11/17/world/americas/peru-sterilizations/?hpt=wo_t3.

268. Paul Lombardo, "Eugenic Sterilization Laws," Image Archives on the American Eugenics Movement, http://www.eugenicsarchive.org/html/eugenics/essay8text.html.

269. *Buck v. Bell*, 274 U.S. 200 (1927), Cornell University Law School, Legal Information Institute, https://www.law.cornell.edu/supremecourt/text/274/200.

270. "Buck v. Bell," Wipedia.org, the Wikimedia Foundation, https://en.wikipedia.org/wiki/Buck_v._Bell.

271. Ibid.

272. Interview with Elaine Riddick on Maafa 21, available at maafa21.com.

273. "Compulsory Sterilization," Wikipedia.org, the Wikimedia Foundation, https://en.wikipedia.org/wiki/Compulsory_sterilization#cite_note-67.

274. Amnesty International USA, "Women in Indonesia & East Timor: Standing Against Repression," December 13, 1995, 15–16, 23. Cited in Mary Meehan, "How Eugenics and Population Control Led to Abortion," MeehanReports.com, http://www.meehanreports.com/how-led.html.

275. Elizabeth Liagin, "East Africa: The Truth about Foreign Aid," Information Project for Africa newsletter, March 2000, 2, 4 & 1. Quoted in Mary Meehan, "How Eugenics and Population Control Led to Abortion," MeehanReports.com, http://www.meehanreports.com/how-led.html.

276. Liu Yin (pseud.), "China's Wanted Children," *The Independent* (London), Sept. 11, 1991. Quoted in Mary Meehan, "How Eugenics and Population Control Led to Abortion," MeehanReports.com, http://www.meehanreports.com/how-led.html.

Chapter Seven

277. This summary of Kinsey's research is taken from David Kupelian, *The Marketing of Evil* (Nashville: Cumberland House Publishing, 2005), 133.

278. Caleb Crain, "Alfred Kinsey: Liberator or Pervert?" NewYorkTimes.com, October 3, 2004, http://www.nytimes.com/2004/10/03/movies/03crai.html?pagewanted=print&position=&_r=0.

279. Judith A. Reisman, "Crafting Bi/Homosexual Youth," *Regent University Law Review*, 14:283, p. 313. http://www.drjudithreisman.com/archives/regent.pdf.

280. Sue Ellin Browder, "Kinsey's Secret: The Phony Science of the Sexual Revolution," May 28, 2012, Crisis Magazine, http://www.crisismagazine.com/2012/kinseys-secret-the-phony-science-of-the-sexual-revolution.

281. Christopher Turner, "Hugh Hefner in six volumes," *The Guardian*, July 16, 2010, http://www.guardian.co.uk/books/2010/jul/17/hugh-hefner-playboy-biography.

282. Hollie McKay, "Hugh Hefner: Obama Should 'Get Out of the Wars,' FDR Was Best President," FoxNews.com, August 2, 2010, www.foxnews.com/entertainment/2010/08/02/hugh-hefner-obama-wars-fdr-best-president/#ixzz2LGca0glK.

283. Carrie A. Pitzulo, *Bachelors and Bunnies: "Playboy" Magazine and Modern Heterosexuality, 1953–1973* (Chicago: University of Chicago Press, 2011), 225–30.

284. Ibid.

285. Judy Parejko, "The 40th Anniversary of 'No-Fault' Divorce," Sep. 5, 2009, Catholic Exchange, http://catholicexchange.com/the-40th-anniversary-of-%E2%80%9Cno-fault%E2%80%9D-divorce.

286. "Social Indicators of Marital health and Well-Being: trends of the Past Five Decades," National Marriage Project, University of Virginia, Figure 5, http://www.stateofourunions.org/2011/social_indicators.php#divorce.

287. Albert Mohler, "No-Fault Divorce–The End of Marriage?" AlbertMohler.com, March 7, 2005, http://www.albertmohler.com/2005/03/07/no-fault-divorce-the-end-of-marriage-4/.

288. "Social Indicators of Marital health and Well-Being: trends of the Past Five Decades," National Marriage Project, University of Virginia, Figure 8, http://www.stateofourunions.org/2011/social_indicators.php#cohabitation.

289. "Number of sexual partners in lifetime," National Survey of Family Growth, Centers for Disease Control, http://www.cdc.gov/nchs/nsfg/abc_list_n.htm#numberlifetime.

290. "Unmarried Childbearing," Fastats, Centers for Disease Control, http://www.cdc.gov/nchs/fastats/unmarry.htm.

291. CDC Fact Sheet, "Incidence, Prevalence, and Cost of Sexually Transmitted Infections in the United States," Centers for Disease Control, http://www.cdc.gov/std/stats/STI-Estimates-Fact-Sheet-Feb-2013.pdf.

292. Catharine A. MacKinnon, *Feminism Unmodified: Discourses on Life and Law* (President and Fellows of Harvard College, 1987), 99.

293. Ibid.

294. George Weigel, "The Libertine Police State," NationalReview.com, February 13, 2012, http://www.nationalreview.com/articles/290842/libertine-police-state-george-weigel.

295. Dorchen Leidholdt, introduction, *The Sexual Liberals and the Attack on Feminism* (Pergamon Press, 1990), xv, footnote 8. Cited in Rene Denfeld,

The New Victorians: A Young Woman's Challenge to the Old Feminist Order.

296. Mehdi Hasan, "Being pro-life doesn't make me any less of a lefty," New-Statesman.com, October 11, 2012, http://www.newstatesman.com/lifestyle/lifestyle/2012/10/being-pro-life-doesnt-make-me-any-less-lefty.

297. John Cowan, *The Science of a New Life* (New York: Cowan and Company, 1871), 275. Cited in Olasky, *Abortion Rites*, 43.

298. John W. Trader, "Criminal Abortion," paper read before the Central Missouri Medical Association, Sedalia, MO, October 6, 1874, Toner Collection, Library of Congress. Cited in Olasky, *Abortion Rites*, 43.

299. Susan B. Anthony. *The Revolution*, July 8, 1869.

Chapter Eight

300. "Forced Abortion in America: A Special Report," the Elliot Institute, http://www.theunchoice.com/pdf/FactSheets/ForcedAbortions.pdf.

301. Vincent M. Rue, et al., "Induced abortion and traumatic stress: A preliminary comparison of American and Russian women," *Medical Science Monitor*; 10(10): SR5–16. http://www.vozvictimas.org/pdf/documentos/rue2004.pdf.

302. Ibid.

303. "Abortion and Depression Part 1," Interview With Theresa Burke of Rachel's Vineyard Ministries, A Zenit Daily Dispatch, March 4, 2006, http://www.ewtn.com/library/PROLIFE/zabortdepr.htm.

304. M Gissler et. al., "Pregnancy Associated Deaths in Finland 1987–1994 — definition problems and benefits of record linkage," *Acta Obsetricia et Gynecologica Scandinavica* 76:651–657 (1997).

305. DC Reardon et. al., "Deaths Associated With Pregnancy Outcome: A Record Linkage Study of Low Income Women," *Southern Medical Journal* 95:8 (2002), 834–41. Cited in "Forced Abortion in America: A Special Report," the Elliot Institute.

306. M Gissler et. al., "Pregnancy Associated Deaths in Finland 1987–1994 — definition problems and benefits of record linkage," *Acta Obsetricia et Gynecologica Scandinavica* 76:651–57 (1997); and M. Gissler, "Injury deaths, suicides and homicides associated with pregnancy, Finland 1987–2000," *European J. Public Health* 15:5 (2005), 459–63. Cited in "Forced Abortion in America: A Special Report," the Elliot Institute.

307. Vincent M. Rue et al., "Induced abortion and traumatic stress: A preliminary comparison of American and Russian women," *Medical Science Monitor*, 10:10, SR5–16. http://www.vozvictimas.org/pdf/documentos/rue2004.pdf. Cited in "Forced Abortion in America: A Special Report," the Elliot Institute.

308. Mollie Hemingway, "Media Censors Forensic Analysis Showing Planned Parenthood Videos Not Deceptively Edited," Oct. 1, 2015, The Federalist, http://thefederalist.com/2015/10/01/media-censors-forensic-analysis-showing-planned-parenthood-videos-not-deceptively-edited/.

309. Kate Scanlon, "Forensic Analysis: Planned Parenthood Videos Are 'Authentic,'" Sep. 29, 2015, The Daily Signal, http://dailysignal.com/2015/09/29/forensic-analysis-planned-parenthood-videos-are-authentic/.

310. Mollie Hemingway, "Media Censors Forensic Analysis Showing Planned Parenthood Videos Not Deceptively Edited," Oct. 1, 2015, The Federalist, http://thefederalist.com/2015/10/01/media-censors-forensic-analysis-showing-planned-parenthood-videos-not-deceptively-edited/media-censors-forensic-analysis-showing-planned-parenthood-videos-not-deceptively-edited/.

311. Anika Smith, "The 'Consequences' of Investigating the Abortion Industry Come Home to David Daleiden," April 6, 2016, The Stream, https://stream.org/consequences-investigating-abortion-industry-come-home-david-daleiden/.

312. Vincent M. Rue et al., "Induced abortion and traumatic stress: A preliminary comparison of American and Russian women," *Medical Science Monitor*, 10:10, SR5–16, http://www.vozvictimas.org/pdf/documentos/rue2004.pdf. Cited in "Forced Abortion in America: A Special Report," the Elliot Institute.

313. Ibid.

314. See David C. Reardon, "Abortion Decisions and the Duty to Screen: Clinical, Ethical, and Legal Implications of Predictive Risk Factors of Post-Abortion Maladjustment," Manuscript based in part on an unpublished paper originally presented at the American Psychiatric Association Annual Meeting May 17–22, 1997, San Diego, CA. www.afterabortion.org/news/Duty2Screen.pdf.

315. See www.theunchoice.com for further information and cases.

316. From "Forced Abortion in America: A Special Report," the Elliot Institute.

317. I.L. Horton and D. Cheng, "Enhanced Surveillance for Pregnancy-Associated Mortality-Maryland, 1993–1998," *JAMA* 285:11 (2001), 1455–59; see also J. McFarlane et. al., "Abuse During Pregnancy and Femicide: Urgent Implications for Women's Health," *Obstetrics & Gynecology* 100: 27–36 (2002). Cited in "Forced Abortion in America: A Special Report," the Elliot Institute.

318. "Leading Causes of Death in Females United States, 2013." Centers for Disease Control and Prevention, http://www.cdc.gov/women/lcod/2013/index.htm.

319. Kimport K, Foster K, Weitz TA, "Social sources of women's emotional difficulty after abortion: lessons from women's abortion narratives," *Perspectives on Sexual and Reproductive Health*, 43:2 (June 2011),103–9. http://www.ncbi.nlm.nih.gov/pubmed/21651709.

320. Wanda Franz, "New Study Examines Familial Context of Choice to Abort," National Right to Life Committee, Feb. 15, 2009, http://www.nrlc.org/News_and_Views/Jan09/nv011509.html.

321. Priscilla K. Coleman et al., "Predictors and Correlates of Abortion in the Fragile Families and Well-Being Study: Paternal Behavior, Substance Use, and Partner Violence," International Journal of Mental Health and Addiction 7:3 (July 2009), 405–22.

322. Vincent M. Rue, "'The Hollow Men': Male Grief & Trauma Following Abortion," United States Conference of Catholic Bishops, Washington, D.C., http://old.usccb.org/prolife/programs/rlp/rue.pdf.

323. Kate Pickert, "What Choice?" *Time*, Jan. 14, 2013, http://www.time.com/time/magazine/article/0,9171,2132761,00.html#ixzz2LO2njBQy.

Chapter Nine

324. "Current Contraceptive Use in the United States, 2006–2010," Centers for Disease Control and Prevention, National Health Statistics Reports, Number 60, October 18, 2012, http://www.cdc.gov/nchs/data/series/sr_23/sr23_029.pdf.

325. "Use of Contraception in the United States: 1982–2008," US Department of Health and Human Services, Centers for Disease Control and Prevention, National Center for Health Statistics, 15, http://www.cdc.gov/nchs/data/series/sr_23/sr23_029.pdf.

326. L.B. Finer and M.R. Zola, "Unintended pregnancy in the United States: incidence and disparities, 2006," *Contraception*, 84:5 (Nov. 2011), 478–85, http://www.guttmacher.org/pubs/journals/j.contraception.2011.07.13.pdf.

327. L.B. Finer et al., "Reasons U.S. women have abortions: quantitative and qualitative perspectives," *Perspectives on Sexual and Reproductive Health*, 37:3 (2005), 110–18. Cited in "Facts on Induced Abortion in the United States August 2011," Guttmacher Institute, http://www.guttmacher.org/pubs/fb_induced_abortion.html.

328. "Abortion: A Civilised Debate," http://www.youtube.com/watch?v=gL-JK88QObrI.

329. Bernard Nathanson, *The Hand of God* (Washington, D.C.: Regnery Gateway, 1996), 89–90.

330. *The Abortion Problem* (The Williams & Wilkins Co., 1944, publishing the proceedings of a 1942 conference), 28.

331. Christopher Tietze and Sarah Lewit, "Abortion," *Scientific American* 220:23 (Jan. 1969). Cited in "What About Illegal Abortions?" Abort73.com, last updated June 20, 2012, http://www.abort73.com/end_abortion/what_about_illegal_abortions/.

332. Mary Steichen Calderone, "Illegal Abortion As a Public Health Problem," *American Journal of Public Health* 50:7 (July 1960), 949, http://www.ncbi.nlm.nih.gov/pmc/articles/PMC1373382/pdf/amjphnation00308-0022.pdf.

333. Ibid.

334. "Abortion Surveillance — United States, 2003," Centers for Disease Control, Nov. 24, 2006, http://www.cdc.gov/mmwr/preview/mmwrhtml/ss5511a1.htm.

335. "Traffic fatalities fall in 2014, but early estimates show 2015 trending higher," National Highway Traffic Safety Administration, http://www.nhtsa.gov/About+NHTSA/Press+Releases/2015/2014-traffic-deaths-drop-but-2015-trending-higher.

336. Steven Ertelt, "Autopsy Proves Planned Parenthood Killed Woman in Botched Abortion," LifeNews.com, Sep. 11, 2012, http://www.lifenews.com/2012/09/11/autopsy-proves-planned-parenthood-killed-woman-in-botched-abortion/.

337. "Carhart Patient Dead From Horrific 33-Week Abortion Injuries," OperationRescue.org, Feb. 8, 2013, http://www.operationrescue.org/archives/carhart-patient-dead-from-horrific-33-week-abortion-injuries/.

338. Maryclaire Dale, "Dr. Kermit Gosnell's Abortion Clinic: Women Say Abortions Left Them Sterile, Near Death," HuffingtonPost.com, Jan. 23, 2011, http://www.huffingtonpost.com/2011/01/23/dr-kermit-gosnells-abortion-clinic_n_812701.html.

339. Steven Ertelt, "Kermit Gosnell Drugged, Tied Up Woman Before Forced Abortion," LifeNews.com, Jan. 24, 2011, http://www.lifenews.com/2011/01/24/kermit-gosnell-drugged-tied-up-woman-before-forced-abortion/.

340. "New lawsuit: Planned Parenthood forced, botched abortion," Alliance Defending Freedom, Feb. 20, 2013, http://www.adfmedia.org/News/PRDetail/7995.

341. Ken Kolker, "Woman: Botched abortion nearly killed me," WOODTV.com, Feb. 19, 2013, http://www.woodtv.com/dpp/news/target_8/Woman-Botched-abortion-nearly-killed-me.

342. Dec. 27, 2012, letter from Jeffrey Lewis, Director of Public Safety, Muskegon Fire Department to Dr. Robert Lewis Alexander, Women's Medical Services Building, http://woodtv.triton.net/news/mfd-womanmedserv-letter-122712.pdf.

343. Mark Crutcher, *Lime 5* (Denton, Texas: Life Dynamics, Inc., 1996), 208–9.

344. "Physical Risks: Life-Threatening Risks of Abortion," Elliot Institute, http://www.theunchoice.com/pdf/FactSheets/PhysicalRisks.pdf.

345. J.M. Dolle et al., "Risk factors for triple-negative breast cancer in women under the age of 45 years," *Cancer Epidemiology, Biomarkers and Prevention* 18:4 (2009), 1157–66. Cited by Dr. Angela Lanfranchi in "Abortion as a Cause of Breast Cancer," presentation at National Press Club, Dec. 4, 2012, http://www.slideshare.net/tjfjustice/lan-franci.

346. See "Epidemiologic Studies: Induced Abortion and Breast Cancer Risk, Updated September 2012," Breast Cancer Prevention Institute, http://www.bcpinstitute.org/FactSheets/BCPI-FactSheet-Epidemiol-studies.pdf.

347. Angela Lanfranchi, "Abortion as a Cause of Breast Cancer," presentation at National Press Club, Dec. 4, 2012.

348. Freda McKissic Bush, "What Has 40 Years of Abortion Done to America? Medical Aspects of Abortion on Women's Health," Abortion Media Summit presentation, National Press Club, Washington, DC, Dec. 4, 2012.

349. H.M. Swingle et al., "Abortion and the Risk of Subsequent Preterm Birth: A Systemic Review with Metanalysis," *Journal of Reproductive Medicine* 54 (2009), 95–108. Cited in Freda McKissic Bush, "What Has 40 Years of Abortion Done to America? Medical Aspects of Abortion on Women's Health," Abortion Media Summit presentation, National Press Club, Washington, DC, Dec. 4, 2012.

350. "Study finds increased risk of prematurity and low birth weight in babies born after three or more abortions," Aug. 30, 2012, http://www.eshre.eu/ESHRE/English/Press-Room/Press-Releases/Press-releases-2012/Babies-born-after-three-or-more-abortions/page.aspx/1675.

351. Larry Lader, "The Abortion Revolution," *The Humanist* (May/June 1973), 4. Cited in "Impact of Abortion on Society," Life.org.nz., http://www.life.org.nz/abortion/abortionkeyissues/impact-on-society-abortion/Default.htm.

352. Patricia Coleman et al., "Associations between voluntary and involuntary forms of perinatal loss and child maltreatment among low-income mothers," *Acta Paediatrica* 94:10 (Oct. 2005), 1476–83, http://www.ncbi.nlm.nih.gov/pubmed/16299880.

353. Michael J. New, "Abortion Promises Unfulfilled," The Public Discourse, the Witherspoon Institute, Jan. 23, 2013, http://www.thepublicdiscourse.com/2013/01/7630/.

354. "United States Abortion Rates, 1960 – 2013," Wm. Robert Johnston, JohnstonsArchive.net, http://www.johnstonsarchive.net/policy/abortion/graphusabrate.html.

355. John and Barbara Willke, *Abortion: Questions and Answers* (Cincinnati, Ohio: Hayes Publishing Company, 2003), 283.

356. Philip G. Ney, "Abortion and Child Abuse: Which is Cause, Which is Effect?" David Mall and Walter F. Watts, editors, proceedings of the conference "Psychological Aspects of Abortion," sponsored on Oct. 31 and Nov. 1, 1978, by the Stritch School of Medicine, Loyola University, Chicago, Illinois; published by University Publications of America. Quoted in Brian Clowes, *Pro-Life Encyclopedia*, chapter 41 (American Life League, 1995), http://www.ewtn.com/library/PROLENC/ENCYC041.HTM.

357. Philip G. Ney, "Clinician's View: Relationship Between Abortion and Child Abuse," *Canadian Journal of Psychiatry* (July 1979), 610–20. Quoted in Brian Clowes, *Pro-Life Encyclopedia*, chapter 41 (American Life League, 1995), http://www.ewtn.com/library/PROLENC/ENCYC041.HTM.

358. Erica Jong, "If Men Could Get Pregnant, Abortion Would be a Sacrament," HuffingtonPost.com, Jan. 21, 2008, http://www.huffingtonpost.com/erica-jong/if-men-could-get-pregnant_b_82467.html.

359. "Abortion Risks: A list of major physical complications related to abortion," http://afteraortion.org/1999/abortion-risks-a-list-of-major-physical-complications-related-to-abortion/.

360. Ibid.

361. "Higher Death Rates After Abortion Found in U.S., Denmark, and Finland," the Elliot Institute, http://afteraortion.org/2012/higher-death-rates-after-abortion-found-in-u-s-finland-and-denmark/.

362. "Abortions Increase Risk of Maternal Death: New Study," the Elliot Institute, http://afteraortion.org/2012/multiple-abortions-increase-risk-of-maternal-death-new-study/.

363. "Abortion Four Times Deadlier Than Childbirth," the Elliot Institute, June 3, 2000, http://afteraortion.org/2000/abortion-four-times-deadlier-than-childbirth/.

364. Priscilla K. Coleman, "Abortion and mental health: quantitative synthesis and analysis of research published 1995–2009," *British Journal of Psychiatry* 199 (2011), 180–6, http://bjp.rcpsych.org/content/199/3/180.abstract.

365. "Huge 2011 study: Abortion and mental health: quantitative synthesis and analysis of research published 1995–2009," American Association of Pro-Life Obstetricians and Gynecologists, http://www.aaplog.org/complications-of-induced-abortion/induced-abortion-and-mental-health/huge-new-study-abortion-and-mental-health-quantitative-synthesis-and-analysis-of-research-published-1995-2009/.

366. "Abortion and Substance Abuse Link Often Overlooked, Women's Health Review Reports," the Elliot Institute, Jan. 20, 2005, http://afterabortion.org/2005/abortion-and-substance-abuse-link-often-overlooked-womens-health-review-reports/.

367. "Risk of Psychiatric Hospitalization Rises After Abortion," the Elliot Institute, Sep. 22, 2003, http://afterabortion.org/2003/risk-of-psychiatric-hospitalization-rises-after-abortion/.

368. Bryan C. Calhoun, "40 Years of Abortion"; see slide 12 of PowerPoint presentation, http://www.40yearsafterabortion.org/dr-byron-c-calhoun-md/.

369. Philip G. Ney, "Siblings of People Dying in Abortions Suffer Depression," LifeNews.com, July 27, 2011, http://www.lifenews.com/2011/07/27/siblings-of-people-dying-in-abortions-suffer-depression/.

370. Anita H. Weiner and Eugene C. Weiner, "The aborted sibling factor: A case study," Clinical Social Work Journal, 12:3 (Fall 1984), 209–15, http://link.springer.com/article/10.1007%2FBF00759918?LI=true.

371. Elizabeth Leis-Newman, "Miscarriage and loss," *Monitor on Psychology* 43:6 (June 2012), American Psychological Association, http://www.apa.org/monitor/2012/06/miscarriage.aspx.

372. Catherine T. Coyle, "Men and Abortion: A Review of Empirical Reports Concerning the Impact of Abortion on Men," The Internet Journal of Mental Health, 3:2 (2007).

373. Ibid.

374. Catherine T. Coyle, "Men and Abortion: Psychological Effects," http://www.menandabortion.net/MAN/pdf/men_abortion_summary_table.pdf.

375. "A Father's Testimony: I was a coward," Priestsforlife.org, http://www.priestsforlife.org/postabortion/casestudyproject/casestudy760.htm.

376. "Reflection from a father," Priestsforlife.org, http://www.priestsforlife.org/testimonies/document-print.aspx?ID=2692.

377. Account relayed to the author.

378. Vincent M. Rue, "'The Hollow Men': Male Grief & Trauma Following Abortion," US Conference of Catholic Bishops, 2008, http://old.usccb.org/prolife/programs/rlp/rue.pdf.

379. Ibid.

Chapter Ten

380. "The internet porn 'epidemic': By the numbers," TheWeek.com, June 17, 2010, http://theweek.com/article/index/204156/the-internet-porn-epidemic-by-the-numbers.

381. Statement on abortion from the Book of Discipline of The United Methodist Church, http://www.umc.org/site/apps/nlnet/content.aspx?c=lwL4KnN-1LtH&b=5066287&ct=6467539.

382. Marvin Olasky, "Telling the Truth: How to Revitalize Christian Journalism," http://www.worldmag.com/world/olasky/truth12.html.

383. Frederica Mathewes-Green, "How should churches handle the delicate issue of abortion when nearly one-fifth of women who get abortions are sitting in our pews?" ChristianityToday.com, Jan. 18, 2011, http://www.christianitytoday.com/biblestudies/bible-answers/spirituallife/sittingourpews.html?start=1.

384. Rachel K. Jones, Lawrence B. Finer, and Susheela Singh, "Characteristics of U.S. Abortion Patients, 2008," Guttmacher Institute, 9–10, http://www.guttmacher.org/pubs/US-Abortion-Patients.pdf.

385. "Estimated Median Age at First Marriage, by Sex: 1890 to the Present," US Census Bureau, http://www.census.gov/hhes/families/files/ms2.csv.

386. Robin Marantz Henig, "Why are so many people in their 20s taking so long to grow up?" *New York Times*, Aug. 18, 2010, http://www.nytimes.com/2010/08/22/magazine/22Adulthood-t.html?_r=0.

387. "Young Men and Women Differ on the Importance of a Successful Marriage," Pew Research Center, April 26, 2012, http://www.pewresearch.org/daily-number/young-men-and-women-differ-on-the-importance-of-a-successful-marriage/.

388. Hannah Rosin, "The End of Men," TheAtlantic.com, July/August 2010, http://www.theatlantic.com/magazine/archive/2010/07/the-end-of-men/308135/.

389. S. T. Karnick, "Girly Men: The Media's Attack on Masculinity," Salvo.org, http://www.salvomag.com/new/articles/salvo4/4karnick.php.

390. "The Feminization of the American male," RedState.com, http://archive.redstate.com/blogs/bs/2008/jun/13/the_feminization_of_the_american_male

391. Laura Schlessinger, *The Proper Care and Feeding of Marriage* (New York: HarperCollins, 2007), 3.

392. Spectrum, National Public Radio, May 11, 1990. Cited in Mark Crutcher, *Lime 5: Exploited by Choice* (Denton, Texas: Life Dynamics, Incorporated, 1996) 175–6.

393. Thaddeus M. Baklinski, "Researcher: Economic Impact of Abortion in U.S. Since 1970 - $35 to $70 Trillion," LifeSiteNews.com, Oct. 21, 2008, http://www.lifesitenews.com/news/archive//ldn/2008/oct/08102109.

Chapter Eleven

394. Patrick F. Fagan, "The Effects of Pornography on Individuals, Marriage, Family, and Community," Marriage and Religion Research Institute, Dec. 2009.

395. CDC Fact Sheet: Incidence, Prevalence, and Cost of Sexually Transmitted Infections in the United States, http://www.cdc.gov/std/stats/STI-Estimates-Fact-Sheet-Feb-2013.pdf.

396. "Why Abstinence?" Medical Institute for Sexual Health, https://www.me-dinstitute.org/2012/08/why-abstinence/.

397. Mélanie Berliet, "15 Married Men Who Cheated Reveal What It's Like to Have an Affair," July 8, 2015, Thought Catalog, http://thoughtcatalog.com/melanie-berliet/2015/07/15-married-men-who-cheated-reveal-what-its-like-to-have-an-affair/.

398. Stephen Davis, *Walk This Way: The Autobiography of Aerosmith* (Dogeared Publishing, reprint edition, 2003), 275.

399. Steven Ertelt, "Unreleased Michael Jackson 'Pro-Life' Song 'Abortion Papers' Now Out," LifeNews.com, Sep. 24, 2012, http://www.lifenews.com/2012/09/24/unreleased-michael-jackson-pro-life-song-abortion-pa-pers-now-out/#sthash.wWYbsqIB.dpuf.

400. David Bereit and Shawn Carney, *40 Days for Life: Discover What God Has Done . . . Imagine What He Can Do* (Cappella Books, Kindle Edition, 2013), Kindle Locations 1917–21.

401. Account relayed to the author.

402. Frances Moore Lappe, "Beyond the scarcity scare: reframing the discourse of hunger with an eco-mind," *The Journal of Peasant Studies* 40:1, 219–238, esp. pg. 221 ["The world food supply comes to about 2800 calories each day for every person on Earth, enough to make us all chubby (FAOSTAT 2011b)."] http://www.tandfonline.com/doi/pdf/10.1080/03066150.2012.70 8859 .

403. Catherine T. Coyle, "Men and Abortion: Finding Healing, Restoring Hope," Knights of Columbus Supreme Council, 26, http://www.kofc.org/un/en/re-sources/cis/cis334.pdf.

404. Account relayed to the author.

405. David Bereit and Shawn Carney, *40 Days for Life: Discover What God Has Done . . . Imagine What He Can Do* (Cappella Books, Kindle Edition, 2013), Kindle Locations 389–92.

406. Ibid., Kindle Locations 410–13.

407. Account relayed to the author.

408. Eric Metaxas, *Amazing Grace: William Wilberforce and the Heroic Campaign to End Slavery* (New York: HarperCollins, 2007), xiv.

409. Ibid.

410. William Hague, *William Wilberforce: The Life of the Great Anti-Slave Trade Campaigner* (London: HarperPress, 2007).

411. Eric Metaxas, *Amazing Grace: William Wilberforce and the Heroic Campaign to End Slavery* (New York: HarperCollins, 2007), 30.

412. "Sickly shrimp of a man who sank the slave ships," *The Sunday Times* (London: The Times), March 25, 2005.

413. Eric Metaxas, *Amazing Grace: William Wilberforce and the Heroic Campaign to End Slavery* (New York: HarperCollins, 2007), xv.

414. Ibid., xvi.

415. T.C. Hansard, printer, *The Parliamentary history of England from the earliest period to the year 1803* XXIX (London: T.C. Hansard, 1817), 278.

416. Eric Metaxas, *Amazing Grace: William Wilberforce and the Heroic Campaign to End Slavery* (New York: HarperCollins, 2007), xv.
417. Eric Metaxas, *Amazing Grace: William Wilberforce and the Heroic Campaign to End Slavery* (New York: HarperCollins, 2007), xiii.

Index

R

About the Author

Author, speaker, and business leader Brian Fisher is the cofounder and president of Human Coalition, a nonprofit organization dedicated to rescuing children and families from abortion using compassion, grace, technology, and data.

Though Brian graduated from college with a degree in music and recorded various musical projects, his eclectic career has spanned other verticals as well. He started his adventure in Pennsylvania, working in media and broadcasting. He then moved into financial securities, serving as the executive vice president and partner of a fast-growing brokerage and asset-management firm. A large international media nonprofit asked him to join their team as president, so Brian and his family relocated to Florida in the mid-2000s.

Texas called next, and Brian became COO of a marketing agency in the Dallas area. He started Human Coalition as a volunteer, part-time effort in 2009 and then joined the organization full time as its president in 2012. Human Coalition is now one of the largest, most innovative life-affirming organizations in the country.

Brian is a Certified Financial Planner and the author of four books and numerous articles. He and his wife, Jessica, have been married for over two decades and have two teenage sons. Brian and Jessica love Jesus, each other, their kids, Human Coalition, and the Pittsburgh Steelers.